## Pilgrim Spirit

John Taylor is a minister of the United Reformed Church and was President of the URC History Society from 1992–5. He is the editor of the current URC *Service Book* and the author of *Come Wind Come Weather*, a Lent book celebrating John Bunyan. Now retired, he lives in Minehead.

Helena McKinnon is a minister of the United Reformed Church working in the area of spirituality, leading retreats and work-shops. She is also Free-Church Chaplain at Bristol University.

Other titles in the *Rhythm of Life* series

RHYTHM of LIFE

SERIES EDITOR: BISHOP GRAHAM CHADWICK

# PILGRIM SPIRIT

*An introduction to*
*Reformed spirituality*

JOHN H. TAYLOR
with
suggested exercises
by
HELENA McKINNON

Foreword by Terry Waite

CANTERBURY
PRESS
Norwich

© John Taylor and Helena McKinnon 1999

First published in 1999 by The Canterbury Press Norwich
(part of SCM-Canterbury Press Ltd, a member of the Hymns
Ancient & Modern group of companies, a registered charity)
St Mary's Works, St Mary's Plain
Norwich, Norfolk, NR3 3BH

British Library Cataloguing in Publication Data

A catalogue record for this book is available
from the British Library

ISBN 1-85311-246-1

Typeset by David Gregson Associates, Beccles, Suffolk and
printed in Great Britain by Biddles Ltd, Guildford and
King's Lynn

# Contents

# Acknowledgements

The authors and publisher gratefully acknowledge permission from the following: Faber and Faber for quotations from T. S. Eliot, *Little Gidding* and *The Waste Land* from *Plays and Poems of T. S. Eliot*, 1969; Jill Jenkins for a quotation from her hymn 'Living God, your joyful Spirit' in *Rejoice and Sing*, Oxford University Press, 1991; J. M. Dent & Sons for a quotation from R. S. Thomas, *Collected Poems 1945–1990*; Dover Publications Inc. for reproducing the Celtic Knot from Ed. Sibbett Jr., *The Celtic Design Coloring Book*, 1979; quotations from the Bible are from the *New International Version*, copyright 1973, 1978, 1984 by International Bible Society. Permission has been sought for quotations from *John Bunyan, The Pilgrim's Progress*, ed. N. H. Keeble, published by Oxford University Press, 1984.

Kenneth C. Lawson kindly allowed us to quote from his *Spirituality – Forming and Reforming* (1995) which can be obtained from Ecumenical Spirituality Programme, Scottish Churches Open College, 18 Inverleith Terrace, Edinburgh EH3 5NS (price: £6.30, inc. postage and packing). The Revd Dr J. Philip Newell kindly gave permission to quote from *The Pilgrimage of Return* (unpublished), much of which appears in *One Foot in Eden* (SPCK, 1998).

We are much indebted to a number of people who have given us unstinted help. The Revd Dr Raymond Brown, for many years Principal of Spurgeon's College, read the script, though not the Exercises, making valued suggestions, corrections and raising questions. Mandy Adams also read the script and from the point of view of a lay person and a teacher of English suggested many improvements. The Bishop of Bath and Wells, the Rt Revd James Thompson, the Principal of Westminster College, Cambridge, the Revd David Cornick, and the Revds Dr John Newton, Margaret Nuttall and Dr R. Buick Knox have provided information. Neil and Eva Garrod, together with Ann Webber of Cannington URC, helped with several matters in chapter II. John's wife, Betty, has given much encouragement and helped with the proofreading. The staff of Dr Williams's Library have provided the expert and friendly service for which they are renowned. Finally, we are delighted that Pamela Pavitt has done the cover illustration and Terry Waite the Foreword.

JHT
HM

# Foreword

Some time ago I was invited to make a short television programme. I agreed and travelled with the producer to my home county of Cheshire. Just outside Macclesfield we stopped at a remarkable house. In the last century an earlier owner had laid out his garden following the journey recorded by Bunyan in *Pilgrim's Progress*. Over the years the garden had become overgrown but the new occupants had carefully restored it so that once again visitors could travel along the route planned and designed by careful gardeners so many years ago. As I stepped gingerly across the Slough of Despond and passed through the little Wicket-gate the story of Christian pilgrimage written so graphically by John Bunyan came flooding back to me.

Christians of all traditions value an understanding of pilgrimage. In part it represents a journey during which individuals and communities seek a closer union with God. The different traditions within the Christian Faith have expressed pilgrimage in a variety of ways. The peculiar history and culture of the various traditions have often shaped these expressions, so, for example, those within a Catholic framework might represent their pilgrimage by reciting the Stations of the Cross or by travelling to a holy place. Reformed Christians would make an equally colourful and exciting journey by use of story and parable as Bunyan so powerfully illustrates.

The various forms of institutional expression of Christianity have certainly shaped the spiritual pilgrimage of Christian men and women across the ages but they have not contained it. Nor can any one tradition claim exclusive rights to spiritual wisdom, although some have tried. The Christian pilgrimage has been deeply influenced by politics and historical events but at the heart of pilgrimage there has always been the desire to know, love and serve God and to grow into the freedom offered by Christ.

The *Rhythm of Life* series attempts to look at spirituality from many seemingly different viewpoints. In this book, following the pathway trodden by Bunyan, the authors not only give a particular insight into the Reformed understanding of spirituality but they also provide an opportunity for the reader to make his or her own personal journey into God.

Just as the new owners of the house with the Bunyan garden cleared away the weeds and restored that which had been neglected for so long, so perhaps this little book might introduce many to a well-trodden pathway and also to a pilgrimage that will be unique for each and every one of us.

Terry Waite CBE
Suffolk 1999

# Series Introduction

*'Wisdom is to discern the true rhythm of things:*
*joy is to move, to dance to that rhythm.'*

This series of books on various traditions of Christian spirituality is intended as an introduction for beginners on the journey of faith. It might help us discover a truer rhythm as something of the experience of those who follow any particular tradition resonates with our own.

Too much can be made of the distinctions between the different expressions of Christian spirituality. They all derive from the experience of what God has done and is doing in us and among us. While emphases differ, their validity is their congruence with the good news of Jesus Christ in the scriptures. As the various instruments in an orchestra make their special contribution to the symphony, so we delight in the extra dimension that each tradition brings to the living out of the Christian faith.

The present wide interest in spirituality seems to indicate that, in the midst of all the current uncertainties that we meet in contemporary life, despite its relative comfort and technological advance, there is felt a need to reconnect with our spiritual roots and find a deeper purpose for living.

Each volume offers an introduction to the essential elements of the particular spiritual tradition and practical guidance for shaping our everyday lives according to its teaching and wisdom. It is an exploration into the way that spiritual practice can affect our lifestyle, work, relationships, our view of creation, patterns of prayer and worship, and responsibilities in the wider world.

Many books, of course, have been written in all of these areas and in each tradition classic commentaries are available which can never be surpassed. The aim of this series is to meet the needs of those searching for or beginning to explore the journey inward into their inmost being and outward to relationship with people and the whole of creation.

Before reading this book in manuscript, the idea of traditional Reformed spirituality conjured up for me an image of narrowness, heavy, negative moralism and a bias to the left-hand side of the brain, the logical and intellectual, rather than the imaginative and intuitive. I am thankful to have been shown otherwise.

The Word is central but so are the Sacraments of Baptism and the Lord's Supper. Feeling has a place as well as reason. Study of the Word is combined with meditation on the Word. The author points out that both the Reformers and Ignatius Loyola drew on a common source. Spiritual guidance is given not only through sermons but through one-to-one pastoral counselling.

In these more ecumenical times, there has been a meeting of minds and hearts. People are appreciating the riches in each others' traditions and what we hold in common. A clear example of this is seen in Helena McKinnon's exercises at the end of the chapters. While coming out of the Reformed tradition, they bear a close resemblance to those in other volumes such as Peter Tyler's *The Way of Ecstasy: praying with Teresa of Avila* and Philip Newell's *The Book of Creation: the practice of Celtic spirituality.*

Bishop Graham Chadwick
Salisbury
December 1998

# Preface

The Reformed tradition of spirituality has been practised for over four centuries by people of all sorts and conditions, many of them very busy with family and business commitments which demanded most of their time and energy. It has been open to all equally, whether ordained to the ministry of the Church or lay, serving in the world. Indeed, it is more concerned with one's attitude to life, the way one thinks and what one believes, than with particular methods of prayer and meditation, though these are by no means unimportant. It urges us to search and find God in life's rich pattern of light and dark shapes and colours.

When first I agreed to be a contributor to this series, my subject was to be John Bunyan's *The Pilgrim's Progress*. However, I was soon persuaded to broaden it to reflect Reformed spirituality, a much greater challenge. Having only about a year for the work and not living near a library with the specialized books I needed, I have been obliged to limit my scope. Bunyan's masterpiece remains as our guide-book for pilgrimage and its itinerary we shall follow, though not in detail, but to this I shall be adding references and quotations from some other English Reformers as well as Luther and Calvin. Many of the works I am making use of are not in print and only found in very old libraries. There are treasures in them but they lie hidden away like those our age is beginning to rescue from the depths of the sea where lie wrecks without number. As the authors will only be known to a handful of historians I have provided brief biographies in Appendix 2. It should not be supposed that the quotations are typical of this literature, which is generally stereotyped and tedious.

The Reformed tradition of spirituality is alive and growing stronger. It is based on the Bible and prayer, the Church and action. Sadly, churches and ministers have too often taken it for granted and not given it the care and attention required for it to flourish. Moreover, the modern Church has treated its history and heritage very lightly. This book is a modest attempt to help inquirers and novices to appreciate how the past may give reassurance and inspiration to the present.

Quotations from Calvin's *Institutes of the Christian Religion* (for short, his *Institutes*) are taken from the first translation into English by Thomas Morton in 1561, which proved worthy of many editions over two centuries. I have used a 1578 copy. This translation was what the English Reformers would have used.

It sounds pedantic to keep saying *The Pilgrim's Progress* and nowadays we drop 'The' from the title.

The suggested exercises to chapters 1–7 are the work of the Revd Helena McKinnon without whose initiative, enthusiasm and encouragement this book would never have appeared.

John H. Taylor

## A Note Concerning the Suggested Exercises

The suggested exercises have their basis in Scripture and have been included to remind the reader of the centrality of the Word of God in the Reformed tradition. They are not offered as an exegesis on Scripture but as a way of breaking open the Word that engages the imagination. Just as John Bunyan's Christian had his Bible continually at his side, so it is the intention of these reflections to act as an accompaniment.

When we look with new eyes upon ancient texts all kinds of hidden treasures begin to reveal themselves. It is hoped, therefore, that the reader will find benefit from exploring the texts and exercises chosen. It is precisely in daring such an adventure that we discover the pilgrim spirit common to us all.

Helena McKinnon

# I

# Then and Now

## Where Are You Going?

Canada? Cornwall? Crete? Holidays are, next to the weather, about the commonest subject for light conversation. Holidays provide highlights in very mundane lives. Once upon a time it was the pilgrimage which was the adventure of a lifetime. Most of us feel an urge to visit distant places, have adventures, meet new friends, enjoy freedom from the usual chores and feel invigorated. To all this, pilgrimage added the joy of reaching a holy destination.

I knew a man, a questioning, hesitant Christian, who resigned his post, much to the dismay of his friends, and trekked out to India on a spiritual quest. A year later he returned and took up life more or less where he had left off. We asked him what he had learnt in the East and he told us he had been advised to return home and seek what he was after in the roots of his own tradition. He was like the medieval knight who rode far and wide in search of the holy grail, only to discover it back home where he had overlooked it. In T. S. Eliot's words, 'the end is where we start from'.[1]

Church historians in the last half-century have been digging into the roots of the Reformed tradition. *Roots that Refresh*, published in 1991, is one of Alister McGrath's contributions to this research; it is a scholarly yet lively evaluation of the theology and spirituality of the Reformers. His complaint is that our churches have lost their interest in history – their 'long-term memory, in favour of a time-scale that spans at best a generation'. What we need, he says, is 'to recapture that sense of evangelical simplicity, creativity, freshness and vivacity which later orthodoxy often unwittingly seems to have forfeited'.[2]

## Roots

The roots of our tradition go back to the sixteenth century, to the Protestant Reformation. It is a mistake to imagine that this was the sole work of religious enthusiasts such as Martin Luther and John Calvin. Half of Europe was waiting for a signal to rise and teach the proud, corrupt Church a lesson. Rulers were eager to cut ties with Rome; landowners and merchants envied the wealth of Religious Orders; scholars sought freedom from censorship; priests longed to marry; more-over, there was a growing demand for the Church to reform its worship, preaching and organization. Luther's role was to give the signal and furnish the theological and spiritual momentum for change.

In 1517 he invited debate on the practice of selling Indulgences (pardons for the deceased) by nailing to the church door at Wittenberg 95 theses (debating points). He hoped the Church would reform itself; he had no idea of becoming Europe's leading Reformer.

Luther's teaching sprang from his own painful experience. He began by studying law, rejected it and entered an Augustinian monastery, eventually becoming a lecturer at the new University of Wittenberg. The regime in the monastery, which aimed at personal holiness, cast Luther into prolonged depression. From this he was saved by the Vicar-General, Johann von Staupitz, who directed him to study the Scriptures closely and read Augustine. 'It was through you', Luther was to say of Staupitz, 'that the light of the Gospel began first to shine out of the darkness of my heart.'[3] About the same time he also began studying some of the German mystics and Dutch Brethren of the Common Life. As he lectured to students on Romans and Galatians he became increasingly aware of the difference there was between the Church's understanding of God's grace and what is to be found in the New Testament.

In fact, Luther experienced a conversion. Medieval society accepted harsh discipline at all levels as the norm. To discover that God was not like the lords and fathers met with in everyday life, but was full of grace and understanding for weak human beings, forgiving them and encouraging them with his Spirit when they trusted him, brought him feelings of liberation and joy. Peace with God was beyond human endeavour, but Christ crucified readily offered it to those who wanted to leave their old ways behind and follow him.

Soon Luther's publications were spreading across Northern Europe. Quite independently, however, in 1519 the Council-appointed priest at Zurich, Ulrich Zwingli, began lecturing on the Bible, attacking current doctrines such as Purgatory and the Invocation of Saints.

Encouraged by the City Council, he replaced the Mass and sacramental system with simpler services; he abolished priestly celibacy and got married himself. He died in battle defending his canton. The reforms were repeated in some other cantons in Switzerland. While Lutheranism held sway in many German states and was exported to Scandinavia, Calvinism from Geneva took hold of the Netherlands, parts of Hungary, Western Germany and, through John Knox, Scotland, where the Church of Scotland began a chequered career in 1560. The Reformation in England and Wales proceeded in instalments. First, under Henry VIII from 1534, then under Edward VI and lastly under Elizabeth I from 1559. A considerable number of Reformers felt that the reforms had not gone far enough and wanted a fourth stage, bringing the Church into line with Geneva. They earned the nickname, 'Puritans'.

## Always Changing – Always Reforming?

Change is inevitable. The Reformers were well aware of it and they coined a phrase which is still in use today: *semper reformanda*. Literally it means 'always to be reformed,' i.e. requiring reformation; however, it is popularly paraphrased, 'always reforming'. This applies to the Church and the churches; it could also apply to the individual pilgrim. History shows, however, that there has been more change than reformation.

This is not a book about theology or history but they cannot be ignored when digging into our roots. Theological doctrines which were compelling a few centuries ago no longer attract attention, yet our roots are in them. Little is now heard about Justification by Faith and even the Priesthood of All Believers, which is invoked from time to time, hardly rouses excitement, as once it did. Calvin's doctrines of Total Depravity, Predestination and Election seem to us like dinosaurs. Yet they deserve respect. They fortified the Pilgrim Fathers tossing on the cruel Atlantic and they stirred those they left behind to fight for freedom and parliamentary democracy. So then, we will take a brief look at some of the principal tenets which inspired the Reformers and still carry weight among many today.

The Reformation was inspired by returning to Scripture, finding in the Bible an authority superior to that of the organizational Church. The authority of the Bible springs from the revelation of God's grace enshrined in it, his faithfulness and saving purposes which reach a climax in the Gospel, with the birth, life, crucifixion and resurrection of Jesus Christ, furthered by the gift of the Holy Spirit. Both Luther and Calvin realised that the Scriptures vary in quality and importance and were careful to interpret them wholistically. Sadly, following generations took a short-cut and used them like lawyers with their books, seeking proof-texts for verbal battles. Things changed but it was hardly reform.

Only a few die-hard conservatives incline to treat the Bible in this way nowadays and, on the other hand, some liberals do little more than decorate their own humanistic convictions with the odd glance at Scripture. Most people of the Reformed tradition heed both Scripture and the world's situation and try to relate them fruitfully.

To discern God's Word (or message) for ourselves two things are necessary. First, there is the guidance of the Holy Spirit. We need sight which is beyond our own faculties; inspiration which comes from God. It is not foreign to life; poets, artists and others experience something akin to it. Reformers have always recalled with delight what John Robinson, the Pilgrim Fathers' pastor, is reported to have said to them when they sailed off to America: 'he was very confident the Lord had more truth and light yet to break forth out of his holy word.'[4]

Second, fully to understand the Bible requires education. Thus, the Pilgrim Fathers, within a short time of arriving in New England, had founded Harvard. Again, when those who refused to keep to the Prayer Book and accept episcopacy were excluded from universities in England, they set about establishing academies for the education of ministers and the laity. We live in a time when education is under threat, for the emphasis is all on training. Specialization tends to divide us. Thought and reason have been seriously demoted. The pressure is on our feelings – in entertainment and religion. The Reformed tradition has tried to balance feeling and reason; both must unite for wholeness.

The next important doctrine of the Reformation concerned the nature of God, a true Father. God freely forgives those who realise their sinfulness and long for righteousness, who are truly repentant, through the atoning sacrifice of Christ on the cross. He treats them as righteous children. They cannot justify their lives before him; to attempt to gain God's favour and earn salvation by one's own efforts is mistaken. This doctrine goes by the name: 'Justification by (or through) Faith'. Like a football it has been kicked around down the years. One side has displayed on their strips 'Works' and the other 'Faith'. And no one has won! The furore is, perhaps, dying down and at last people are beginning to understand that God looks for both faith and action. In our situation, if the planet Earth is to be saved from ruin the human race has an enormous task before it and our lifestyle is going to have to change, and yet, to be realistic, it is going to take more than we can do to avert disaster.

The world is very short of people with faith and hope for the future. As John 6:18 says, belief is the most important act anyone can offer. Those with a sound faith in God, who has always been and always will be the Saviour, are lights in the darkness.

Puritans have ever been noted for their keeness on the moral life. Had we been able to sit through an hour-long Puritan sermon we should doubtless have heard at least an allusion to Justification and also some moralising. Good deeds and good behaviour were the fruits of faith and proof of salvation. If, in the course of the sermon, our attention wandered and we looked about us discreetly, our eyes would certainly have rested a while on the prominent display of the Ten Commandments which adorned the walls of places of worship. Anyone whose behaviour let Christ down incurred the censure of both the church authorities and the congregation. Nor was an extravagant life-style approved; what was praised was simplicity.

It is hard for us to imagine what a revolution the doctrine of the Priesthood of All Believers brought about. At last the laity were no longer second-class spiritual citizens. Now people were directly responsible to God for their consciences. Ordinary occupations could be seen as vocations. And laymen could play important roles in the government of the Church. Sadly, in the last century the doctrine was hijacked by individualism and religion has since been deemed a private affair.

Calvin's classical structure has suffered from change and decay. A few have attempted to restore it, albeit on new lines. I have never, for example, heard a preacher declare that he believed in Total Depravity (of the human race) but a good many have come close to it, citing the gross wickedness the twentieth century has produced: world-wide war, ethnic cleansing, etc. They have also pointed to the basic self-interest pervading most individuals' attitudes and interests, despite the fact that a good many think they are following Christ. Certainly, in dealing with people, in trying to put into practice the second Great Commandment, to love one's neighbour as oneself, it is prudent to bear in mind the universality of sin – e.g. pride, fearfulness, deviousness and weakness – and to be prepared to forgive.

Calvinism and Predestination are like identical twins in many minds. This would never occur to someone reading Calvin's *Institutes* but subsequent generations tended to make something of a god of it. It underpinned Justification and Election. 'The Lord knows those who are his' (2 Timothy 2 : 19). 'He has chosen us ... before the creation of the world' (Ephesians 1 : 4). 'God has mercy on whom he wants to have mercy, and he hardens whom he wants to harden' (Romans 9 : 18). These are among the texts you would have heard again and again in parish churches and meeting houses. When it came to sorting out the sheep from the goats, however, preachers became extremely cautious. Apart from the obvious sinners whom society condemned, people were left to find out for themselves what category they were in and this caused individuals untold misery as they examined and re-examined their hearts and consciences, seeking assurance. It is a strange fact that Puritans cherished freedom greatly but never felt sure whether it was genuine. In the freedom-loving days of Victoria Predestination had to bow out of the pulpit.

There has been, then, much change and some reform since the time of Luther and Calvin. Where their claims were exaggerated – the Papacy alarmed them – time has exposed it and much has been discarded. But they were asking the right questions about our relationship to God and these we still keep asking. While it is true that the gospel is ever the same and Christ is the same and God's love is ever active, our pilgrimage into it for each of us is a fresh experiment in faith. We should not be content to copy saints who have gone before us; we are called, and promised help, to create a spirituality serving God in our age.

## The Pilloried Puritans

The family of Reformed churches is spread around the world, and calls itself by names: Reformed, Presbyterian, Congregational and others, e.g. Church of Scotland. It has all the variety expected in an extended family. We shall dwell on one strand, developed in England, namely Puritanism. It is part of the Anglican Communion's heritage; the Methodists are greatly indebted to it through John Wesley himself, who was really a late-flowering Puritan, while the Baptists, emanating from the early days of the Reformation, were part of it.

Nowadays the word 'puritan' is a term of abuse applied to anyone who delights in being a killjoy. Admittedly the Puritans deserve a bad press for a lot they did. They were severe and unwisely tried to make everyone else the same. But they cannot have been so inhuman as they have been portrayed or else crowds would not have thronged their weekday lectures to hear the Word of the Lord, nor would they have won the hearts of large majorities of people in many towns and cities. With the Commonwealth experiment came serious disappointment and disillusion. People began wanting their sports and festivals back and when the rulers went so far as to execute the king, the country began to fear for the future.

Puritanism, therefore, has to carry a stigma, though the Royalists should share guilt for fomenting the Civil War.

The Restoration of the monarchy did not sweep Puritanism into oblivion. There was a sound spirituality in it which survived years of repression and persecution. It later emerged as Dissent (with the appearance of Presbyterians, Congregationalists/Independents and Baptists) so called because of its origin in 1662 when nearly two thousand clergy of the Established Church refused to conform to *The Book of Common Prayer* and were ejected from their livings just before their tithes from farmers in their parishes were due to them!

Besides references to Luther and Calvin we shall dip into several writings of the Puritans, which date from Tudor to Hanoverian times. Nor shall we forget John Wesley or Jonathan Edwards (in North America). Special mention must be made of John Bunyan. His *The Pilgrim's Progress* is the best-known of all books of the Puritans, having been translated into many languages. It is not a children's book despite its superficial resemblance to one. Its strength lies in its liveliness, humour, common-sense and spirituality. It will provide the framework of our chapters – the itinerary of the pilgrimage.

## John Bunyan

Bunyan was born into an artisan family at Elstow, near Bedford, in 1628, the third year of Charles I's reign. After a little rudimentary education he was out on the roads of Bedfordshire, bearing a very heavy anvil (it would remind him of his sins one day!), following the tinker's trade. It was a skilled occupation: he would have been relied upon to provide and service equipment for dairies, breweries, inns and the kitchens of great houses. Two years he spent soldiering in the Parliamentary Army, glad not to see active service, but sad and shocked when a comrade was shot dead at his side. Before his twentieth birthday he was married, a common occurrence in those days; by 30 he was a widower with four children, one of them blind.

His conscience began to trouble him after a fearsome sermon delivered by his vicar. Among his wife's few books he found Arthur Dent's *Plaine-man's Pathway to Heaven* (1601), which, along with the Bible, led him into a severe and protracted depression, which was only relieved when he met John Gifford, minister of a Bedford congregation, a remarkable man, having been both an army officer and doctor before turning to the ministry. In 1654 Bunyan joined his church and was soon being encouraged to preach. He gave his first sermon when he was 31.

The year before the Restoration, 1659, Bunyan married again. His new wife, Elizabeth, turned out to be a courageous and resourceful woman. This she needed to be for the following year John was arrested and imprisoned for leading a conventicle (a clandestine religious meeting). He was to spend the best part of the next twelve years in gaol. John did his best for his family, which grew to seven children, by making boot-laces, but they must have depended for support on friends. Sometimes the prison regime was lax and John could go home for periods, and sometimes it was grim, fellow-prisoners dying of plague around him. At these times he was desperately miserable. Brave Elizabeth went to London on horseback to plead for her husband's release, but in vain.

In gaol Bunyan took up writing. In his lifetime he produced a vast output, most of it making dreary reading to us today: long-winded theological works, mostly controversial in that century. However, he did venture to write some pieces with a touch of the novel about them, though the novel as we know it had yet to be invented. *Pilgrim's Progress* he wrote to while away the hours. Not till many years later was he persuaded to publish it.

Another side to Bunyan's character is his organizing ability. When toleration dawned and release was imminent, Bunyan set about the task of establishing dissenting congregations in the East Midlands, writing to people all over the place urging them to obtain licences to hold meetings for worship.

When he left prison he was chosen to succeed Gifford at the Bedford church, which was both Congregational and Baptist. As time went by he became a popular preacher and was much in demand in London and the South-East. No doubt his cheerfulness, good sense and earnestness accounted for this; he had friends among cultivated people as well as humble, ordinary folk. The theologian John Owen was one of his close friends. Riding back to London from Reading where he had been called to settle a church dispute, he got soaked in a storm, caught a chill which turned to pneumonia, and he died on 31 August 1688. He was buried with the élite of Dissent in Bunhill Fields, London.

Since those times life has changed dramatically – have people changed much? We live longer, but are we any better? Knowledge has grown immensely, but has wisdom grown at all? Reading the Puritans is like watching a period piece on stage. The setting and the costumes are different, so is the language, yet the characters are recognizable and familiar. Their hopes and fears, troubles and joys we know. There is a sympathy between us.

*Suggested Exercise: Owning our Inheritance*

*Again, the kingdom of heaven is like a merchant looking for fine pearls. When he found one of great value, he went away and sold everything he had and bought it.* (Matthew 13 : 45f.)

### The Bright Field

I have seen the sun break through
to illuminate a small field
for a while, and gone my way
and forgotten it. But that was the pearl
of great price, the one field that had
the treasure in it. I realize now
that I must give all that I have
to possess it. Life is not hurrying

on to a receding future, nor hankering after
an imagined past. It is the turning
aside like Moses to the miracle
of the lit bush, to a brightness
that seemed as transitory as your youth
once, but is the eternity that awaits you.

*R. S. Thomas*[5]

What do you treasure and what do you seek?

Quite ordinary Puritans kept diaries and notebooks in which they recorded impressions of their spiritual pilgrimage: experiences, events, verses of Scripture, quotations and comments on books, prayers (often composed by themselves), etc. I have found this useful. It helps one stop, think and unravel one's thoughts; it serves as a resource and it induces gratitude to God. Why not try it?

## 2

# Making a Start

### In a Mess

We arrive on pilgrimage – a motley company, starting from different places, coming by different routes.

Bunyan's 'hero', Christian, we find 'clothed in Raggs', with 'a great burden on his Back', reading his Bible, weeping, crying out: 'What shall I do?' He wanders in the fields alone. He looks 'this way and that way, as if he would run', but it would be a long time before he started on the way. On the other hand, his wife, Christiana, makes up her mind in a few hours but it has taken the death of her husband to make her think seriously about it. Her young friend Mercie plans to accompany her a short way as a gesture of good-will and ends up going all the way! Bunyan is true to life.[1]

Bishop Jim Thompson tells us what happened to him in *Stepney Calling*. One Christmas Eve he could not face going into church with friends. He called himself 'a practising unbeliever' and was, in any case, 'a bit the worse for drink'. He went and sat on a tombstone and gazed up at the frosty, starry sky. He wondered about himself and his life.

Then I had a sense of God telling me that, in

spite of all my failures and sins, He loved me and was encouraging me to search for him. I remember getting on my bike and riding home singing because I sensed that I was free and that a new life was opening up for me.[2]

Bunyan had been deeply troubled by his sinful past. The sin that most grieved him was swearing, a sin that we would not class among the worst, but he tells us that he had gained a bad reputation in Bedford for shocking people with his eloquent profanity. Obviously his gift with words was emerging, though to ill ends. For some time he imagined he was damned for good because he had, out of devilment, cursed the Holy Spirit, until it was explained to him that this unforgiveable sin refers not to careless words but a malign spirit which dismisses good as evil (Matthew 12:22–32). But there was much more to his remorse. He was profoundly unhappy with the prevalent way of life. Christian tells his wife that it is the way to ruin.

This may strike chords with us at the end of the twentieth century. Embryonic pilgrims may surface from the unstable, chaotic, sexual, domestic and economic waters of modern life, seeking good air to breathe. Oh to be free from the constant pressures and strains of the rat-race! Money! Money! Debt and anxiety! Those dreams of self-fulfilment nurtured by fond parents and inspiring teachers doomed to failure. But could it be that the way of the spirit is the true path to be yourself?

While the Puritans knew nothing of our over-complicated civilization they were not total strangers to our troubles and we find Richard Baxter describing the rat-race:

> what riding and running, what scrambling and catching there is for a thing of nought while eternal rest lyes by neglected. What contriving and caring, what fighting and bloodshed to get a step higher in the world than their brethren ... what insatiable pursuit of pleasures.[3]

The economic injustices of our time, which strike our hearts when we see dying children on the TV screen, are not entirely new, as Dent tells us. 'The mighty ones do wrong the weaker.' 'Cruel, oppressing bloud-suckers' and 'pernicious and pestilent vermine,' he calls them.

> I think there was never more of them then in these days ... an Iron Age. It seemeth that the great ones mind nothing else; they are all together set upon oppression. Poore children cry for bread; poore widowes also, and poore fatherless children are found weeping and mourning.

He concludes: 'God doth looke upon them, and will be revenged.'[4] This was the downside of the glorious Elizabethan age and Raleigh's foolhardy adventuring.

In those days they did not have to contend with the scientific and technological revolution which brings us a mixed bag of blessings and curses. We have become impersonal, ant-like in society. Where genetic engineering is going to take us is worrying. The destruction of so much of the natural world, the exploitation of resources and the pollution of earth's protective envelope, resulting in climatic changes, make it more reasonable today than it was in Bunyan's day to prophesy ruin and destruction.

The tragedy is that the nations are not ignorant of these things but lack the will to reform. Churchill was repeatedly warned in Cabinet by Arthur Balfour before Gallipoli that ships had never managed to overcome land fortresses, but the dream of opening the way to Russia was too strong for reason and the disaster-course was endorsed by the Cabinet. Today, no one wants to face hard facts.

Full of melancholy, Christian tumbled into the Slough of Despond; nor could he drag himself out without assistance. At any time on pilgrimage one can get stuck in it. It feels, as T. S. Eliot wrote, as if 'we who were living are now dying'.[5]

Floundering in the bog, one's view of the Church is jaded. The dearth of spirituality among its members fills us with dismay. Has it always been so? Nearly four hundred years ago John Preston was complaining bitterly about churches with the form but not the power of godliness. In them he encountered stubborn women and men who acted 'like Lyons in their families' and were 'false in their dealings'.[6]

The Church's teaching seems a dismal failure. There is great joy at Christmas with carols and candles yet we seem to have great difficulty in believing that God is personal. Who, then, was Jesus? The cross is prominently displayed and the sacrament of the Lord's Supper is

regularly repeated but the preacher rarely convinces us
that he or she has really come to terms with suffering and
evil; sometimes in prayer great claims sound hollow, even
trite. How threadbare a good many acts of worship are;
how superficial charismatic performances seem all too
often. Sadly, one has left services wondering whether that
preacher and those people really had any treasure-store
and any good news to share – they had the form but not
the power of godliness.

It may surprise readers to hear of Bunyan pondering
'whether there was in truth a God or Christ or no' and
asking whether the Bible was written by some politicians
'to make poor ignorant people to submit to some religion
and government'. Perhaps Marx was not quite as original
as we always thought.[7]

Loss of faith in the old ways has led people to look
elsewhere. Zen Buddhism and forms of transcendental
meditation have given a new sense of peace to some. New
Age has attracted those in open revolt against Western
Society. People clutch at ancient beliefs, the occult and
astrology – Hitler was one – but the majority remain
confused and prone to superstition. G. K. Chesterton
observed that 'when people cease to believe in God, they
do not believe in nothing but in anything'.[8]

## Advice – Good and Bad

One sunny day, Bunyan happened to overhear the
conversation of a small group of women. We can imagine
him pausing in his work as he sat nearby and pricking up
his ears, for they were talking about 'the things of God'.
They came from Gifford's church and soon Bunyan was

there, drinking in the preacher's thirst-quenching words. Bunyan would always remember those women, sitting in the sunshine. For him it symbolized the grace of God.

None of us is likely to get far on our spiritual journey without coaching. Books can be a great help. We have mentioned Dent's influence on Bunyan. As a young teenager, Richard Baxter's life was given focus by a popular religious manual known as *Bunny's Resolution*, which, curiously enough, was a Jesuit production adapted for Protestants by Edmund Bunny! Spirituality knows no bounds. A very famous person whose conversion was due to a book was William Wilberforce. Returning from Italy, a friend persuaded him to read Philip Doddridge's *Rise and Progress of Religion in the Soul*, a soul-searching book which went through many editions in the eighteenth and nineteenth centuries. But we also need to resolve doubts and difficulties with advisers we trust and like.

Evangelist in *Pilgrim's Progress* is modelled on Gifford and he characterizes the best kind of Reformed pastor: knowledgeable, wise and watchful. Anything resembling what is termed 'brain-washing' today is foreign to genuine Reformed tradition. We have a brain: we must think for ourselves. There is no pressurizing in Evangelist's counselling. He asks Christian whether he can see the wicket-gate, i.e. is he near to deciding to go the Christian way? 'No,' answers Christian. So Evangelist then asks him if he can see the shining light and, with less than certainty, Christian says, 'I think I do.' 'Keep that light in your eye', advises Evangelist, 'and go up directly thereto.' He is firm and gentle.[9]

However, Christian soon falls under the spell of kindly Worldly-Wiseman, who cautions him not to take a preacher's advice too seriously. Religion is fine, provided it is taken in moderation. Good behaviour is what matters; zeal only leads to fanaticism. Christian tries out the man's advice, only to find that it is lifeless and unsatisfying. Once more he is in distress. He has failed to go directly towards the light.[10] 'We are prone to cast down ourselves, we are accessory to our own troubles, and weave the web of our own sorrow, and hamper ourselves in the chords of our own twining.'[11]

'What doest thou here?' Christian is confronted by ever-watchful Evangelist. After a severe dressing down, as they part, Evangelist kisses Christian and gives him 'one smile'.[12] To the other qualities the Reformed minister must add love and, moreover, be able to express it. Perhaps ministers of Evangelist's quality are few and far between. Nevertheless, others may suffice. Baxter recalls one in his youth who helped him though he was 'of weaker parts than many others but yet did profit me more than most'. What Baxter remembered was that he never spoke of God or of the future life 'but with such marvellous seriousness and reverence as if he had seen the Majesty and Glory which he talkt of'.[13]

Family and friends are all too often less than understanding. They may ascribe the seeker's condition to some mental aberration. David Brainerd, the New England pioneer missionary to the Indians, remarks that anyone showing signs of conversion will be said to be suffering from 'melancholy vapours disturbing the brain'.[14] Bunyan treats the situation humourously. Christian's relatives supposed 'some frenzy distemper had got into his head' and 'got him to bed', but when he showed no signs of improvement, they 'thought to drive away his distemper by harsh and surly carriages to him: sometimes they would deride, sometimes they would chide, and sometimes they would quite neglect him'.[15] He became lonely and miserable.

> For none so lone on earth as he
> Whose way of thought is high and free
> beyond the mist, beyond the cloud,
> Beyond the clamour of the crowd.[16]

Baxter asks his readers whether 'they do not feel sometimes a strong impression to retire from the world and draw near to God?' and counsels them not to disobey 'but take the offer and hoist up your sails while this blessed wind may be had'.[17] Talking with candidates for the ministry and also with people seeking confirmation or baptism, one frequently hears stories resembling those of Augustine of Hippo, who kept putting off the day of decision, and Jonah, who sought desperately to escape the call of God, but as Psalm 139 reminds us, there is no escape: God's hand is upon us.

The wicket-gate symbolizes conversion in *Pilgrim's Progress*. It refers to changing one's mind, changing direction, adopting different aims for one's life. Bunyan's skill as a pastor is revealed in that Christian at this stage of development only feels sure of the goodwill of God. He did not grasp the high-priestly role of Christ yet. When he asks the gate-keeper if he can be relieved of the burden of guilt which distresses him he is told to be patient. 'As to the burden, be content to bear it, until thou comest to the place of Deliverance'.[18] This is all the more astonishing because at a later stage in the tale Christian realises that the gate-keeper, called Good-will, was none other than Christ, whom he had failed to recognize![19] In the last century Revivalists, eager to win souls, imposed a particular pattern on conversion: the act whereby a penitent surrendered his or her will to Jesus Christ. In earlier times it seems to have been recognized that total conversion is a long process, often life-long. Nevertheless the first milestone passed is a satisfying sign of decision after wearisome indecision.

## Suggested Exercise – Seeking Stillness

*Be still and know that I am God.* (Psalm 46 : 10a)

Sometimes it is the hardest thing to silence the noisy clamour of the world outside – and the world within. There are so many intrusive sounds, so many perplexing thoughts that vie with each other for our attention. Even at prayer we are rarely at ease enough simply to let go and *let God* ... We love to fill every space with words, as though by our eloquence we may somehow command a better hearing. Certainly within the Reformed tradition with its emphasis on the Word, there has been a fearful love of wordiness. At last we are learning to redress the balance.

Weaving silence into worship, public and private, opens up the way to thoughtful reflection. We are discovering that we need that sacred space more and more.

> Drop thy still dews of quietness
>   till all our strivings cease;
>   take from our souls the strain and stress,
>   and let our ordered lives confess
>   the beauty of thy peace.[20]

In *Pilgrim's Progress* Christian has to contend with many disturbing sights and sounds on his way to the Celestial City. His journey is continually interrupted by encounters with loud people who, for the most part, leave him exhausted and out of sorts. It is only when he receives quiet guidance from sound counsellors such as Evangelist and the Interpreter or enjoys the gentle regime of hospitality at the Palace Beautiful, that he regains spiritual equilibrium.

It is so important for our spiritual well-being to find a place apart – a secret place – where we can spend time in quietness, if for no other reason than to recharge our batteries. To be able to still body, mind and spirit is something that we need to cultivate as part of our practice of prayer.

This simple exercise is intended to do just that.

- First, light a candle as a visual focus.
- Sit comfortably on a chair, with feet touching the floor, back straight and hands resting gently in the lap.
- Become aware of your body as you breathe slowly in and out.

- Notice the little changes that occur in the rising and the falling of breath.
- After a few minutes tighten the fists as you breathe in, and hold the tension for a few seconds.
- On breathing out, release the hands and let them quite naturally fall back open.
- Repeat several times until you feel relaxed.
- Now begin to repeat the phrase, 'Be still and know that I am God' until it becomes part of the steady rhythm of your breath.
- Then employ the following technique:

> Be still and know that I am God
>     (*Silence*)
> Be still and know that I am God
>     (*Silence*)
> Be still and know
>     (*Silence*)
> Be still
>     (*Silence*)
> Be

- Remain in the stillness for as long as it is helpful.
- Open the eyes and turn again to the candle.
- Tune yourself once more to your surroundings.
- Read Mark 4 : 35–41 – Jesus stills the storm.

# 3

# Getting a Grounding

## The People of God

A Christian is not like a piano – a fine solo instrument. Christians are members of an orchestra, supporting one another. In a church it becomes possible to grow spirituality and mature, to join in team work and fulfil one's own special role; it helps one to survive in hard times.

The supreme work of a church is to worship God, and the pilgrim needs to feel at home in it. The spiritual temperature at an act of worship has to be right, neither too hot nor too cold. It may come as a surprise to a newcomer to find, instead of a reverent silence before worship, the opposite: hubbub. People greet each other, embrace, laugh and chatter while children run amok. Nor will the newcomer be ignored in a truly friendly church. Only as the time for the Call to Worship approaches will the social sound subside. The Puritans spoke of gathering for worship on the Sabbath as the spiritual market day, an opportunity for the community to come together. Today's impersonal, often lonely way of living, requires just such a community.

Matthew Henry said the purpose of the Sabbath was twofold: to honour God and promote the good and happiness of ourselves.[1] This would well describe how we see worship today. There are instances of worship turning into a quasi-entertainment or perhaps a class for religious education. But elsewhere it may just seem like a time-honoured rite, out of touch with today's life and culture. In such cases the twofold purpose is not achieved. Ideally, worship should be both serious and happy as well as being useful and good. Hymns, songs and other music generate congregational praise and prayer; as Jonathan Edwards said, they 'excite and express religious affections'.[2]

Quite the most important question the pilgrim has to ask about any church is, What does it stand for? It will be apparent in various ways but not least in what is preached. Are we hearing the good news of God's grace? The thrust of the Reformation was to return for inspiration and authority to the Bible, read as a whole, the source of faith, hope and our mission in the world. Most Reformed churches display an open Bible prominently during worship as a reminder of our roots. If, however, the sermon proves to retail the preacher's own musings on life or validates fashionable social trends, the pilgrim may look at the open Bible on its lonely stand with pity. On the other hand, when the words uttered strike home with something more than human reasoning, projecting biblical truth to engage with our condition, we rejoice.

In Reformed churches the sacraments, Baptism and the Lord's Supper, are characterized by simplicity. Because of this, and because the Lord's Supper is not normally celebrated weekly, outsiders have sometimes assumed that the sacraments are not thought to be of great importance. It has to be admitted that a hundred years ago this was the case. It is not so today, nor was it in earlier times. To worship Christ without the sacraments is like being in the army and never going on parade. The Reformed tradition stands for the Word *and* sacraments, as it also believes in the marriage of reason *and* feeling.

Baptism symbolizes the grace of God through Jesus Christ; thereby we share in his dying and rising and are initiated into the Body of Christ. The Lord's Supper reminds us of what Christ has achieved for us and invites us to renew our acceptance of him and allegiance to him. The English Reformers owed a lot to their Continental tutors. Following Philip Melanchthon, they embraced the covenanting concept of the Lord's Supper, the bread and wine being seals to the new covenant. Ulrich Zwingli's simple memorial service had a strong appeal for it was manifestly contrary to the Roman Mass, with its claim that the real presence of Christ was in the two elements. John Owen, the foremost Calvinist theologian of the seventeenth century, plainly stated: 'this bread doth not contain the body of Christ; the cup doth not contain the blood of Christ; but they exhibit them.' Yet many Reformers, including Calvin and Owen, were dissatisfied with Zwingli's superficiality. Owen asserted: 'Christ is present with us; he doth really tender and exhibit himself into the souls of believers in this ordinance.' It calls for, not just obedience, but delight and thanksgiving, 'a heart full of love'.[3]

Pilgrims who go about seeking a perfect church will surely be disappointed, and if they did find one they would also discover that they were unfit to join it. Bunyan, writing dreamily his *Pilgrim's Progress* from gaol, isolated from the opposite sex, fantasized about the church. Christian is welcomed into it by Discretion, a beautiful damsel, who seems to have forgotten her name for she kisses him and tears stand in her eyes. Other fair ladies with equally virtuous names, Prudence, Piety and Charity, join her to interrogate the newcomer as to his spiritual experience in the ancient manner of Independent churches, before admitting him to full membership. When Bunyan came to write Part II of his masterpiece he was out of prison and he painted a different picture of Christian fellowship with its abundance of unheroic folk, whom he was careful to observe the Lord loves and protects. Alongside Valiant-for-Truth and old Honest we find Ready-to-halt, Dispondencie and Fearing, 'one of the most troublesome Pilgrims'. Yet they all seem happy together. Dancing was, of course, forbidden by strict Puritans. However, in a dream, who could stop it? So we see the company dancing in the road together to music played by Christiana and Mercie![4] In fact it was not always such a jolly fellowship, as the Bedford Church Book reveals. There were wayward members requiring discipline and those who felt offended and left, a process Calvin described as the Lord 'smoothing' the church's 'wrinkles and purging away its spots'. For a fellowship to thrive there has to be what Owen calls 'animating principles'.

> While we are clothed with the flesh we do all things imperfectly; we know but in part, and hence we offend in many things ... Some delight always to dwell upon others' failings; they

deserve no charity themselves. ... Let pity not
envy; mercy not malice; patience not passion;
Christ not the flesh; grace not nature; pardon not
spite or revenge, be the animating principles in
our hearts.[5]

## Christ and His Way

Before becoming a full member of the Body of Christ the
pilgrim will receive some tuition in the fundamentals of
the Church's faith and practice. For centuries this meant
learning the Catechism devised by the Westminster
Assembly in Commonwealth times. Today there is no
prescribed form though various churches have their own
standards and literature designed for catechumens.
Nothing, however, replaces the personal attention of
someone trained to help pilgrims with their difficulties
and inspire their imaginations. In *Pilgrim's Progress* this
takes place in the Interpreter's House and the first thing
the pilgrim is shown is a picture in a dark, almost secret,
chamber, of 'a very grave Person' who 'stood as if it
pleaded with Men, and a Crown of Gold did hang over its
head'. Who was this?[6] Bunyan is not explicit. Pilgrims are
at different stages of development and have to reach their
own conclusions. Perhaps the Apostle Paul is meant since
Bunyan loves quoting him. It has been suggested that the
pastor himself is represented. But may it have been Christ,
as seen in Paul's letters and in Revelation 1? Christ
crucified was the mainstay of Puritan teaching. 'If we
can but teach Christ to our people,' says Baxter, 'we shall
teach them all.'[7] Each pilgrim has to decide individually
the significance of Christ.

An excellent beginning is made by reading the Gospels and letting Jesus' words and actions engage our inmost thoughts. Though they concentrated on Christ and the cross, the Puritans were not unmindful of the Lord's example. Sibbes says, 'Look upon Christ, not only for healing, but as a perfect pattern to imitate.'[8] Of course none of us will copy Christ as a little child copies a parent; what is indicated is to observe his patience, love, mercy, meekness, obedience and contempt for the world, as Isaac Ambrose enjoins us and 'in all these Graces . . . conform to Christ'.[9]

As we study the life of Christ we come face to face with some crucial questions. Was he more than human, as the Bible claims? And there is an underlying question: can a modern person believe in God who is personal? David Blunkett speaks for many people when he states that he believes in 'a Life-Force' but not in a 'tangible way'.[10] What he means exactly by 'tangible' is not clear. God is, after all, Spirit. The alternative to belief in a personal God requires us to believe that the Life-Force by accident produced beings capable of thought and feeling, powers it did not possess itself. In the past the mistake was too often made of supposing God to be like a human being; today we have to be careful not to rule out God's having personal traits among his many attributes. Unless God and human beings have personal dimensions in common, communication is impossible.

Without the personal God the pilgrim's emotional needs cannot be met, and God made these! The weakness of pure Calvinism was its cold intellectualism, but happily plenty of Reformers amended it to conform with their religious experience. For instance, John Preston. It may surprise some readers to learn that before the tragedy of the Civil War King Charles had in his employ a Puritan chaplain who undertook several missions for him. This was Preston and here he expresses feeling,

> If thou be in Christ, there goes out a virtue from him that stamps upon thy heart (an) holy affection that breeds in thee (an) holy fire of love, so that thy heart cleaves to him, thou lovest him with as true, with as genuine, as naturall and as sensible love as thou lovest any friend.[11]

The disastrous period of religious intolerance and strife was followed not surprisingly by the Age of Reason, and Christianity was in danger of losing the warmth of the gospel. One who sought to remedy the situation was Edwards. In his *Treatise concerning Religious Affections* he declares, 'how great is their error who are for discarding all religious affections as having nothing solid or substantial in them'.[12]

Reason and feeling are linked in *Pilgrim's Progress*, and nowhere more clearly than over Christ's atoning death. Although taught about the latter by the Interpreter, Christian is obliged to continue on his way bearing his wearisome burden of sin. Patience is all the advice he receives. In Puritan religion there is no easy, quick solution to sinfulness, no cheap grace. The pilgrim must carry his burden to learn the gravity of sin, both his own and the world's. Not until he feels as Christ did does the day for relief arrive and it is surprising and exciting.

Christian came to an incline crowned with a cross and below there was a grave.

> So I saw in my Dream, that just as *Christian* came up with the Cross, his burden loosed from off his Shoulders and fell from off his back; and began to tumble; and so continued to do, till it came to the mouth of the Sepulcher, where it fell in, and I saw it no more.
>
> Then was *Christian* glad and lightsom, and said with a merry heart, He hath given me rest, by his sorrow; and life, by his death. Then he stood still a while, to look and wonder; for it was very surprising to him, that the sight of the Cross should thus ease him of his burden. He looked therefore, and looked again, even till the springs that were in his head sent the waters down his cheeks.[13]

It was indeed surprising, for Reformed Christians abhorred symbols; these belonged to the old Roman order. Nowadays we are more appreciative of symbols and indeed colour and gesture, to help our pilgrim spirits.

Trials were not however, over for our pilgrim. Sin is never banished while the blood circulates. It has always troubled Christians, made them feel hypocrites, and in earlier centuries particularly, often led them to doubt whether they were saved. Christian idly lost the scroll entitling him to heaven and had to return to retrieve it. Pastors in those days had to labour to reassure the fearful. If we turn to Calvin we find him assuring us that 'the mercy of the Lord would be vain and delusive, if it were only granted for once'. he is certain that 'the merit of Christ' and 'the sanctification of the Spirit' 'is daily bestowed upon us'.[14] What is essential is what direction the person is facing: towards God or away from him.

*Suggested Exercise – Digging for Treasure*

> *Listen to me, you who pursue righteousness*
>   *and who seek the Lord:*
> *Look to the rock from which you were cut*
>   *and to the quarry from which you were hewn;*
> *Look to Abraham, your father,*
>   *and to Sarah, who gave you birth.*
> *When I called him he was but one,*
>   *and I blessed him and made him many.*
>   (Isaiah 51 : 1f.)

In the above text we are presented with an image which suggests that discerning God's will does indeed involve considerable excavation, like quarrying. The prophet invites those 'who pursue righteousness and seek the Lord' to do some serious digging – to begin the task of exploring the firm foundation of faith upon which our forbears built their hopes and dreams. We are given the example of Abraham and Sarah by way of inspiration. Their faith and fortitude made God a living reality, grounded as it was in the experience of grappling with changing circumstance and fleeting fortune. It was their perseverance and staying power amid the trials and tribulations of their day that saw them through to the land of promise. It is that model of 'dedication to the Lord' that we are called to honour and exemplify ourselves.

- Find a stone to act as a focus for reflection. Choose one large enough to hold comfortably in the palm of your hand.
- Sit quietly with it for a few moments.
- Become aware of its weight and form; its colour, texture and patterning.

### Meditation on a Stone

This stone has its own story to tell.
　　It is as old as the hills
　　and holds many secrets.
Long before human beings existed
　　it was already part of the earth,
caught up in the great movement of shifting
　　mountains, being uniquely shaped and moulded
　　by physical forces, so strong and powerful,
　　that it still bears the imprint today.
It has travelled a long way
　　on its journey from below to above
　　and witnessed many changes.
Water, wind and weather have also left their
　　mark – and human kind.
And yet now it has come to light with you,
　　has come to rest in the palm of your hand,
　　to become part of your experience,
　　as a mirror to your own thoughts and feelings.

Its age, strength and resilience
all speak of things eternal and unending,
like faith, hope and love.
There is surely much mystery and majesty here.

- What qualities inherent in the stone do you identify with?
- Recall the times you have felt the 'firm rock' of another's example to bring you encouragement and strength.
- Read Psalm 40 : 1–3.
- Place the stone in some special place as a reminder of those things.

# 4

# In Touch with God

## Prayer and Meditation

Christian's church friends took him to the armoury to be equipped for battles ahead.[1] Reformed preachers delighted in expounding Ephesians 6:13ff. with its breastplates, shields, helmets and swords, to which the apostle adds 'all-prayer'. This imagery has probably lost its glamour for most of us, yet pilgrimage is still a tough struggle for which we must be prepared. Prayer should not be isolated from its context like a church artefact on display in a museum. It integrates one's faith and hope, one's example, mission and witness. As Baxter says, it is 'the breath of a Christian's life'.[2]

From time immemorial people who are serious about spirituality have realised that prayer is a daily activity. 'When thou first openest thine eyes in a morning, pray to God and give him thanks heartily ... and when thou liest down, let that be the last also,' says Perkins,[3] and Bayly is more businesslike: 'Begin, therefore, every day's work with God's Word and Prayer.'[4] At night one should meditate and pray about the day that is over. Time must be taken to do this, says Perkins, for it is the equivalent of oiling wheels and sharpening knives before commencing operations.

However, what happens between rising and retiring is of most consequence, not only to us but to God. So we need to learn to recollect the presence of God from time to time during the busy day. Walking with God was the biblical expression our forefathers used; another was waiting on God, a very meaningful phrase for people who were almost all masters, servants or both. It was (and still is) the careful, skilful and cheerful execution of our duties that pleases God. No one is going to say that recollecting the presence of God is easy but small habits may be acquired which make it easier, such as thanking God for his providence before eating, seeking his blessing when we settle down to tasks and always asking for his help in face of difficult situations.

Rules for prayer, Scripture reading and meditation, which stipulate times and lay down daily exercises are too often beyond the capability of busy, lay people. The Reformers deliberately generalized. Morning and night have from time immemorial been times to remember and praise God but neither is ideal for either quiet reflection or hammering out problems before God. Each of us has to work out our own pattern of devotion and this will vary with our circumstances. Busy people show remarkable ingenuity in finding time as they wait for trains, drive vehicles or walk the dog. However, longer periods in leisure time need to be cultivated; they yield a rich harvest.

Four rules for prayer were laid down by Calvin in *The Institutes*. They tell us nothing about when, where or what to pray; they concentrate on what is even more important, how to pray.

1. Approach God in the right frame of mind, staying very still and quiet, and firmly dismissing 'earthly cares and affections'. Be full of respect for God: we do not 'sportingly talke' with one who is our equal. Later in the chapter he adds that the first prayers we make should acknowledge both our sinfulness for which we need pardon and our thankfulness for all our blessings.[5]

2. Supplications are to be 'earnest yea fervent'. 'Many', complains Calvin, 'for maners sake recite prayers after a prescibed forme.' But Christians must mean what they say.

3. Take care to be truly humble before God. One must 'forsake all thinkinge of his owne glory' and, not trusting to his own wisdom but 'in the abacing of himself' give 'glory wholly to God'.[6] Easily said, not so easily done. For example, someone who has initiated a project prays for the blessing of God upon it, but what does God see? He may see an egoist hungering for praise and popularity. Blindly 'we runne all into love of ourselves' and 'every man thinketh himselfe to have a just cause to advance him selfe'.[7] How persistent the ego is. When we shut the door on him, he reappears and begins opening the window and when we shut that, we hear him descending the chimney!

4. Trust God the Father who is 'favourable and beareth good will' towards us.[8] As we entrust our affairs to solicitors and bankers and our bodies to surgeons and nurses, we must leave all our concerns in the hands of God. Provided we always remember

to pray in the Name of Christ, for his kingdom, not ours, our inadequacy need not bother us too much. Our language is of little consequence to God and the length of our praying may be to our disadvantage! (Matthew 6 : 6). The preachers of previous centuries who loved extended prayers seem never to have read this far in Calvin's *Institutes*.

The necessity of praying in the Name of Christ figured prominently in Reformed teaching. Two points were made. The phrase 'through Jesus Christ our Lord' which occurs frequently at the end of prayers indicates that Christ is the advocate who takes our ineffective efforts and shapes them for presentation to the Father. And secondly, praying and also acting in the Name of Christ, as his servants, are the primary functions of all who have dedicated themselves to God's service. Our personal concerns are not unimportant. Our well-being matters but has to take a secondary place; this is part of losing one's own life for a greater (Mark 8 : 35). Prayers, however, often fall short of this norm and, mercifully, God understands our weakness and helps and blesses us to encourage our faith and love.

Petitions and intercessions constitute the sharp end of prayer. The activities of today and tomorrow, the problems ahead, our hopes and fears, and thinking about the people we expect to be meeting constitute a considerable agenda. But there is much more to be done.

The Priesthood of All Believers is probably more on preachers' lips than any other Protestant doctrine and it is taken to mean that penitents need neither priest nor saint, but Christ alone, to approach God for forgiveness and cleansing. In fact this is only half Luther's teaching: 'priesthood makes us worthy to stand before God and pray for others.' We do not need special 'postures and clothing as we see among men. . . . Rather it consists in the spirit'.[9] The Christian's mission is to try and build bridges between the world and God, its Maker and Saviour (1 Peter 2 : 9). It is an infinitely wide remit, from remembering lovingly those around us with pressing needs to pondering before God on monstrous issues such as unemloyment and global warming. Calvin underlines at length Paul's confession (Romans 8 : 26ff.) that at times we weak beings do not know how or what to pray and have to rely on God understanding the groans the Spirit makes within us. In practice this is all too often the case. Prayers often end by being totally silent before God and waiting on him.

Calvin follows his rules for prayer with many pages of exposition on The Lord's Prayer, our model prayer. This is not the place to summarize it but he emphasizes that saying it daily should warn us against appropriating God for oneself exclusively as one's own Father. 'How great affection of brotherly love ought to be among us' who make this our daily prayer.[10] Alas, Calvin did not mention sisters. His womenfolk caused him a lot of headaches!

With the exception of The Lord's Prayer, set prayers were taboo for the majority of Reformers on the grounds that they did not come from the heart and easily slipped into thoughtless repetition, 'saying your prayers'. Those, however, who stayed within the Church of England in

1662 accepted The Book of Common Prayer and helped to preserve a treasury of prayer. Today both corporate worship and private devotion are often enriched by printed prayers while verses of the Psalms, hymns, songs and poems may be used by individuals to uplift their praise and thanksgiving and deepen their penitence. Hymns are, after all, but musical prayers.

In addition to morning and evening slots for prayer and odd moments in the course of the day, we need more prolonged times for prayer, meditation and reflection. In the past, when towns were tiny, travel was on foot or by horseback, when birdsong, not the roaring of tractors and transistors, accompanied labours in the fields, solitude was the lot of many. In our noisy existence, it has to be sought and cultivated in obedience to the Lord's bidding (Matthew 6 : 6) to find a secret place for communion with God. Some people flee from solitude. Why do they run away from God?

In recent times interest in meditation has mushroomed, stimulated by Oriental practices, and many people have profited from them. Kenneth Lawson warns us, however, that 'searching after newer and more exciting experience' without facing up to one's spiritual condition will prove unsatisfying. The 'integration and wholeness' which the Reformers sought after, we too have to seek.[11] The historian A. G. Dickens assures us that abandonment to a 'vast and cloudy infinity of God' was not what Luther meant by meditation; for him Christ and the gospel was the focus.[12] The Reformers were not interested in the mental techniques of the medieval mystics intent on ascending the ladder of perfection. They sought God's

Word, his message in meditation. The results of meditation are rather quaintly described by Baxter, who, we must remember, used to treat parishioners' ailments as well as their souls:

> As digestion turneth food into chyle (*the product of the gastric organs*) and blood, for vigorous health, so meditation turns the truths received and remembered into warm affection, firm resolution and holy conversation.[13]

How meditation was conducted the Reformers left to groups and individuals to decide, providing they began and ended with prayer. Since the tendency to drowse is a common nuisance, they would advise people to change posture, walk about, write things down, anything to keep alert. The secret place is secret. We all differ and have to find by trial and error what is best for us. We also have to learn how to read and assimilate Scripture.

There is a difference between reading some verses of the Bible day by day in devotions as a reminder of God's Word and reading one or two lengthier passages for the purposes of meditation. Here we may mention that it has been noticed how closely Ignatius de Loyola's *Exercises* are to Reformed practice and recently research has revealed that they both have the same medieval root. Prejudiced as we may think the Reformers were in many ways, they were pleased to employ Catholic spiritual practices where these assisted them. Joseph Hall gave the Puritans a clear method for meditating on the Bible in his *Arte of Meditation* (1606) but it was lifted from the Catholic Jean Mombaer's *Rosetum* (1494) to which

Ignatius's system is also related. In essence the method is to absorb oneself quietly into the biblical text, using reason and imagination to sympathize with it. It is not difficult to do with gospel stories; perhaps rather more difficult to hear Paul dictating one of his letters or Malachi lecturing his hearers; it can be fascinating going into the Temple and hearing the choirs chanting back and forth, one moment exultant, the next plaintive. It should also be noted that Luther, Calvin and others distinguished between those parts of the library we call the Scriptures which are of most value and those that are least, Calvin having a system reminiscent of our one to five star categories for hotels, with the Gospels scoring the highest rating.

Learning to read the Bible is not unlike learning to sing. It is not very difficult to be able to sing simple songs and hymns acceptably; the amateur may be trained to sing anthems and cantatas in a choir; but to go further and sing solo in a Requiem Mass requires long, arduous training. With the Bible the recipe is to enjoy the simple things and gradually increase one's repertoire. While the guides for daily Bible reading and specialized books may be a help – not all are – there is nothing to replace sitting under a knowledgeable and gifted teacher and enjoying discussion with others. Beware, however, of instructors who do not give pride of place to the gospel of grace. It can have heinous consequences. It led Cromwell and his army chaplains into hallowing and imitating the blood-iest chapters of the Old Testament.

In the end we are judged by our fruits. What good comes of all this praying and meditating? In Henry's words, 'we must wait upon God' because 'we have a duty to do, many an opportunity of speaking good words and doing good works'.[14] Dag Hammarskjöld died on a mission for the United Nations in Africa and one of the notes he left behind affirms: 'In our era the road to holiness passes through the world of action.'[15] But what can anyone do who is old and infirm? I recall one such who ministered to all visitors with her sensitive and penetrating questions and smiling encouragement. Some said she had a better understanding of the congregation with whom she could never worship than those who could. Our fathers would be aghast to see how many in our tradition have taken to retreats, even silent ones; they are a haven to storm-tossed pilgrims today. There is, however, a question we have to ask ourselves: whether we are being escapist. In any case, for most of us it is impossible to devote much time for meditation frequently and regularly. It is consoling, then, to have Baxter the spiritual doctor counselling us to concentrate on how we spend our time in meditation for that matters more than how long we spend at it. How people wrong themselves by spending too long delving into their sorrows, mistakes, disappointments and sinfulness. They should enjoy God and all his works. 'Reader, I entreat you, let praises have a larger room in your duties; keep material ready at hand to feed your praise.'[16]

Prayer and meditation, habitually practised, have the side-effect of slowly changing the character; the Spirit is at work within. Henry noted down some of the benefits enjoyed. We learn to be calm and collected, free from 'the care and cumber which attends much serving'. Whatever the nature of the troublesome situation to be faced it will be approached in a relaxed and confident manner. Our Father does not let us down. 'The God we wait upon continually waits to be gracious to us.' Going about our business, all we see and all we meet reveal 'much of God in every creature'. Making things, we 'enjoy the Creator while we are using the creature'.[17] Doing acts of charity or making donations, we seek God's blessing and glory, repressing our own. Preparing to entertain friends we look for God's presence – things have been known to go wrong! Furnishing our homes and looking after them provides us with opportunities to thank God for all his mercies. At this point perhaps we may add a plea for Christians to dedicate their artistic gifts and tastes to the glory of God. Too few of us rebel against ugliness and drabness – we get accustomed to it, like sin – which is obviously contrary to the natural world God designed.

In case any reader feels guilty about not walking with God as much as they might, perhaps a few words from a prayer of Thomas Arnold may be a consolation:

> O Lord, I have a busy world about me: eye, ear and thought will be needed for all my work to be done in the busy world. Now, ere I enter upon it, I would commit eye, ear and thought to thee. Do thou bless them and keep their work thine; such as, through thy natural laws my heart beats and my blood flows without any thought of mine for them, so my spiritual life may hold on its course at those times when my mind cannot consciously

turn to thee to commit each particular thought to thy service.[18]

## Know Thyself

It is no accident that Christian had hardly set out from the Palace – now a new church member – when he met with trouble. First, he had to descend into the Valley of Humiliation, which he did 'very warily, yet he caught a slip or two', and then he had to face the dragon, Apollyon, who told him the painful truth about himself and came near to destroying him. His troubles were not yet over for after that he entered the fearsome Valley of the Shadow of Death. If there is one thing all spiritual teachers would declare in unison it is that pilgrimage is not for weaklings. Nevertheless, Bunyan's pastoral experience showed him that often people who appear rather timid get through these dangerous places unscathed. Christiana and her companions did not stumble as Christian had done. They did not see any monster and, much frightened, they nevertheless passed through the grim Valley of the Shadow safely, protected by their pastor, Mr Greatheart.[19]

Those who suffer the worst in the Valley of Humiliation are those who try to walk tall, superior to their companions. They slip and fall. 'If anyone thinks he is something, when he is nothing, he deceives himself,' says Paul (Galatians 6:3). Let him test himself. 'The more others commend thee for an excellent act, be thou the more humble in thy own thoughts,' says Lewis Bayly.[20] But it is not the wish of God that we remain lying wretchedly on the ground. If we feel depressed and dejected who is to blame but the one with false pride? 'Our owne hearts', remarks Thomas Goodwin, 'are the causes of this darkness.'[21] Sibbes asks us to remember, 'there is a sweetness in reproof'.[22]

Bunyan makes the Valley of Humiliation beautiful; our Lord had his country house here. What will appeal to modern pilgrims is that it is 'free from the Noise and from the hurryings of this Life'.[23]

Sadly, humility, like Cinderella, is ignored, even despised, in modern society, having been confused with dullness, docility and servility. It has had a bad history. For centuries Church and State drilled it into everyone to make sure they kept to their station in life and kept the peace. For true humility we cannot do better than look to Jesus. We see it in his ministry to all sorts and conditions of men (including women and children) but we see it supremely in his birth in a stable and death on a cross. Yet his humility did not stand in the way of his fierce denunciation of the Pharisees or King Herod. While he rode into Jerusalem on a donkey, manifesting humility, his cleansing of the Temple was far from what anyone then or now would call a humble act. Nor did his washing of the disciples' feet, like a slave, conflict with his occasional rebuking them – he was their master and Lord. In this competitive age, when those who fall get trampled upon, we have to witness to Christ's kind of gracious/tough humility.

In Christian literature there is nothing to compare with Bunyan's combat between Christian and Apollyon. The pilgrim's pride is finally pricked. As a lad, Bunyan must have witnessed, even if he did not take part in, the Mummer's Play, which inevitably, to the delight of the crowd, presented St George's fight with the dragon and his victory. In *Pilgrim's Progress* Christian is armed like the saint and faces Apollyon, 'hideous to behold', 'cloathed with scales like a Fish', with 'wings like a Dragon, feet like a Bear', and 'mouth like a Lion', belching out 'Fire and Smoak'. Bunyan embellishes the encounter with a good helping of slapstick wrestling and swordsmanship but the real wound occurs when Apollyon exposes Christian's lingering guilty feelings about his past, showing that his faith in Christ is not absolute, and perceives that Christian's self-confidence is not without pride: 'when thou talkest of thy journey, and of what thou hast heard, and seen, thou art inwardly desirous of vainglory in all that thou sayest or doest?' To this Christian can only reply sheepishly: 'All this is true and much more.' He is not to be defeated, however: 'The Prince whom I serve and honour, is merciful and ready to forgive.' Acknowledging his infirmities, he adds: 'I have groaned under them, been sorry for them, and have obtained pardon.'[24]

Which Christians are most likely to have to face such an encounter? All who aspire to lead, whether great or small. Bishop Jim Thompson describes what occurs:

> The necessity to win battles, the control over other people's lives, the seductive applause, the arrogance of life-style, the external protection against the small indignities, the growing conviction that we are right, and the necessity to

subdue opposition – all these things can lead to a loss of inwardness, and a creation of distance between the successful person and others. ... Slowly, without noticing, the external expression of the self becomes so important that the soul is given in its service.[25]

Down in the Valley Christiana and her friends listen to a boy 'in very mean Cloaths, but of a very fresh and well-favoured Countenance' singing:

> He that is down, needs fear no fall,
> He that is low, no Pride:
> He that is humble, ever shall
> Have God to be his Guide.[26]

Bunyan's description of the Valley of the Shadow of Death is equally vivid. It is 'dark as pitch' and inhabited by 'Hobgoblins, Satyrs, and Dragons' who strike fear into pilgrims with their 'continual howling and yelling'. The pathway is 'exceeding narrow' and there is a deep ditch on one side and a quagmire on the other. Christian resorts to 'All-prayer'. The place reminds him of the valley referred to in Psalm 23.[27]

Some scholars say that what Bunyan was concerned about was doctrinal error. While this may be so, what he describes so vividly is a common experience when we go through a difficult, dark phase of life. All teachers of theology and spirituality must deal with this phase. What Bunyan is gifted to do is to say what it feels like. Whether our fear is losing our job or health or income; whether disruption in the church or firm or home makes us fear the future; whether it's having to stand helplessly by while tragedy unfolds before our eyes, we must not succumb to petrification but by prayer and recollecting God's promises in Scripture push fear back. Mr Greatheart, Christiana's minister, was able to frighten off attackers: it is safest to share troubles and fears with others who may provide what we ourselves lack in dark times.[28]

Goodwin has some remarks that are helpful in his *Childe of Light walking in Darkness*. He notes how dark times thrust us close to God whereas those 'that know not any afflictions in this life often feare God lesse'. Many sufferers have found, as he had, that the experience gave them greater sympathy for others: 'Learn to pitty others. ... Who can doe it better than you, that have experienced the like?' Finally, there is light at the end. God provides comfort when it's over: 'God alone keepes the keys of that cupboard, and alone dispenseth how and when he pleaseth'.[29]

## *Suggested Exercise – Struggling with the Dark*

Struggle is part and parcel of pilgrimage. The authentic encounter with our deepest selves reveals the truth about who we are and whose we are. Just as Christian had to do battle with Apollyon, the gargantuan figure of his alter-ego, so we too must confront the many shadows lurking in our subconscious.

The writers of the Bible did not have our psychological perspective but they could describe the reality of inner turmoil vividly; they also had the awe-inspiring backdrop of the patriarchs and the dramatic tale of God's getting to grips with them.

Read Genesis 32 : 22–32 – enter into the story at your own pace.

For Jacob this self-knowledge comes at a crucial time when his past is about to catch up with him in the shape of his twin brother, Esau, whom he had cheated many years before of his rightful inheritance. At dead of night, beside the water's edge, stripped of his possessions, Jacob arrives at this place of knowing. The encounter leaves its mark, but though hurt, he is also blessed, for within the wrestler's grip he discovers the warm embrace of acceptance. He is given a new name and status.

- Reflect on the 'unknown stranger' who visits you with challenging questions, disturbing your ease.
- In what guise does this figure come?
- Where do you find the grip pressing hardest?
- How do you respond?
- Note all that surfaces within you and begin to explore the thoughts and feelings that arise in the context of God's loving acceptance of you as his beloved child.

# 5

# In the World

## Pilgrims and Strangers

The story of the Pilgrim Fathers emigrating to New
England in the autumn of 1620 and nearly perishing on
the way in the fierce North Atlantic gales is the most
famous in the annals of the Reformed Churches. What
is less well known is that the passengers on board
the *Mayflower* were a very mixed crowd. Besides the
'saints' who were nearly all members of John Robinson's
congregation of exiles in Holland, there were the 'strangers' who were not. Some of them were described as
profane and one ended up on the gallows. In addition
there were, of course, numbers of children, some servants
and a few hired hands. The 'strangers' were on board at
the insistence of the investors to make the venture
commercially viable. The little ship epitomizes the situation in which Christian pilgrims always find themselves:
in the world, among those who are strangers to the faith
and to spiritual values.

Discrimination or worse, persecution, are sometimes
suffered in the world. The Pilgrim Fathers fled from it for
liberty in the New World but they left behind tens of
thousands of their friends to face humiliation. What the
Lord said about taking up the cross (Mark 8 : 34–36) they

knew applied to them. Discrimination against those who would not conform to the Church of England only disappeared towards the end of the nineteenth century. To this day anyone ordained to the ministry of the United Reformed Church has to promise to maintain the truth of the gospel 'whatever trouble or persecution may arise'. Persecution continues to grieve Christians in many places. We, however, are fortunate; all that Christians have to bear is some ridicule and possibly ostracism where they work or live until, by patience and goodwill, they earn the respect of 'strangers'.

Our situation colours our view of the world. When Bunyan was writing his *Pilgrim's Progress* he was still smarting from the biased trial he had been put through, so he drew a Hogarth-like picture of Faithful's trial scene with the jury which condemned Faithful to death comprising men like No-good, Malice, Love-lust, Live-loose and High-mind. When Bunyan came to write the second part of *Pilgrim's Progress*, he was home again. Times had changed and pilgrims were 'acquainted with many of the good people' of Vanity Fair, 'and did them what Service they could'.[1] Neighbours were now more like friends than 'strangers'. Christians, then, must be prepared to take up the cross, though no more desirous of it than our Lord was in Gethsemane.

## Work – Careers and Callings

The pattern of our lives is determined supremely by two factors: our occupations and our marital status, unless ill-health overwhelms us. We shall consider marriage in the next chapter; here we turn our attention to work, which generally takes up a very great part of a person's time, energy and thought. By work we mean not only paid employment but voluntary work, housework, homework – all the diverse tasks which occupy us.

Work began to be seen in a new light at the Reformation, as an aspect of God's will, what he calls us to do, and to do to his glory. The ancient fence between religious and secular duties was torn down. Ploughman and priest, with their different duties, were equally doing the will of God. George Herbert, in his hymn, 'Teach me, my God and King', plainly says nothing is too menial to be done to God's glory:

> A servant with this clause
> makes drudgery divine:
> who sweeps a room, as for thy laws
> makes that and the action fine.

This lofty concept was wrecked on the rocks of the Industrial Revolution. Thousands of people had to spend their lives sweating in dark, wet mines or tending machines in noisy, dusty mills, and preachers were sensitive enough not to declare that such toil was divine. Just a few occupations, in the Church, medicine and education, continued to be regarded as callings and even they are under question nowadays.

Until recent times people had little if any choice in what work they did. Unemployment, on the other hand, was uncommon. Now there is choice, but there is unemployment. In deciding upon a career, anyone who takes to heart the great commandments to love God and one's neighbour will survey the needs of the world and assess their talents – aptitudes, skills, abilities and interests – taking into account the advice of good friends and seeking God's guidance, before reaching a conclusion. Thereafter it will be a case of hard work, proving one's ability and seizing the opportunity that occurs while remaining faithful when all doors seem to shut in one's face.

Implied in the spiritual approach to work is prayer. People, profits, new ideas and perennial problems, all need turning over in the presence of God. Prayer gives a better perspective than thought and discussion alone. It 'sanctifies our common actions to God, and sweetens them, and makes them pleasant to ourselves.' Henry then refers to Colossians 3 : 17, 'do everything in the name of the Lord'.[2]

## The Protestant Work Ethic

The Protestant Reformation brought with it the notion that work was God's will. Did not God give Adam work to do in the Garden of Eden before the Fall (Genesis 2 : 15)? Idleness, then, was anathema. Our unemployment problem would have infuriated the Reformers. In this century the Protestant Work Ethic has been vilified by some, as the Church abetting capitalists in exploiting the workers, and praised by others, such as Mrs Thatcher and President Nixon, for teaching the values that matter for economic health, competition and self-reliance. Both sides have read into the Reformers what they wanted to see there. Before the eighteenth century capitalism was in its infancy and the Industrial Revolution had not been born. It is doubtful if theologians and preachers of those times, who were constantly warning the wealthy against worshipping false gods and treating the poor with contempt, would have spared governments or conglomerates today. Nor did they neglect to balance work with leisure.

## Recreation

In 1869 Matthew Arnold took his generation to task for its boring solemnity. It drilled people in being energetic and determined, in learning concentration and self-control – Puritan virtues – but it had lost sweetness and light, the Greek virtues.[3] The criticism was not without foundation. Indeed, the Puritans reckoned the theatre depraved; art had only limited use and games were a waste of time. Even a hundred years ago such narrow-mindedness was prevalent in some circles. Nevertheless, it is evident from Bunyan's masterpiece, especially Part II, that Puritans managed to enjoy themselves. Pilgrims love to be together, to eat, drink and be merry together. They enjoy playing with children. They rag and tease one another. Indeed, Bunyan got into trouble for mixing fun with religion: 'some say he laughs too loud.'[4] He took no notice. More seriously, Bunyan's folk admire gardens, fine buildings and clothes of good quality. Their most precious pleasure, however, is making music. Even in gaol Bunyan managed to fashion a recorder from the leg of a stool!

In these days it is necessary to exhort people to take enough physical exercise whereas in former days it was hardly apposite, for they were continuously exerting themselves in a multitude of daily chores and even people who could afford carriages and horses in fact were always walking and walking, on business and for pleasure. However, Baxter, writing for the reading public, felt he should warn them 'not to neglect the due care of your bodily health' for 'your body is a useful servant if you give it its due, and no more than its due'.[5] Excellent advice, but do not become a hypochondriac as he tended to be in my opinion. John Downame strikes a chord:

> Neither is recreation onely allowed as lawfull, but also injoined as profitable and necessary. ... For as the strings of a Lute let down and remitted, doe sound sweeter when they are raised again to the full pitch ... so our bodies and minds ... by timely remission will afterwards make more harmonious melody. ... We are not made of God fit instruments of perpetuall motion.[6]

Getting out into the country but away from roads or out in a boat with no telephone provides good recreation, peace. 'When the Flowers appear and the Sun shines warm' it is Prudence's delight to go and listen to the birds singing. They are fine company, she finds, when one feels depressed.[7] Like the Celts, the Puritans often saw God teaching them in nature, something that survived into this century in many a preacher's childrens' talk.

There was nothing, however, to compare to the Sabbath for re-creation. Its objectives were rest from daily work and worship. In this century entertainment has secularized Sunday. In Britain church attendance has dropped dramatically and the pleasures of the weekend are likely to leave both adults and children weary on Monday. John Downame was right: strings need relaxing (Matthew 11 : 28) but have we found the right way of doing it?

Regular worship, especially on the first day of the week, establishes the rhythm of our spiritual life. It helps concentrate our discipleship. Just as committee meetings are valuable in spurring people to fulfil promises and play their part as members of a team, so Sunday worship makes us remember who we are and what we should be doing. We can praise God in a way which we cannot do on our own; we can listen and learn; we can join in the sacrament of the body and blood of Christ – something we may never do on our own!

Of course, there are good pilgrims who seldom if ever attend Sunday worship because of work or incapacity. It is a great pity. It makes the spiritual life all the more difficult for them. However, when they can come, or when others visit them and share the Word and sacraments with them, their appreciation is obvious in their smiles and handshakes.

## Following Christ

When Peter went to Caesarea to visit Cornelius, the centurion, he told the folk who had gathered there about Jesus and described his work in Galilee quite simply: he 'went about doing good' (Acts 10 : 38). Followers of Christ have tried to copy his example.

But today 'do-gooding' has a bad press. Yet how can communities get on without it? Of course it is not praiseworthy when conducted in a manner which is patronizing, interfering or bossy – quite the opposite of Jesus' way. Nor is it when it is done not to please God but to win praise and honour (Matthew 6 : 1–4). Surely, anyone who seeks God in spirit only, and who makes no effort to go about doing good, cannot find him. Once more Baxter: 'Do not only take occasions of doing good when they are thrust upon you, but study how to do all the good you can.'[8]

The women of Bunyan's congregation made clothes for the poor of Bedford. In his simple but vivid language he says, 'their Bellys and Backs blessed' them and thus 'Christ's name ... was like to live in the world'.[9]

The Reformers also encouraged generosity and hospitality. As refugees abroad, many had been recipients of it in Mary's reign. This work has to be regarded not so much as a duty to be fulfilled as an act of love done for others and for God, reflecting Christ's work.

Sometimes we do not feel like it. We are like Lord Chesterfield, though seldom so open as he, who admitted, 'Nobody can be more willing and ready to obey orders than I am, but then I must like the orders.'[10] Humble, prayerful discipleship will lead us past the milestone where we find to our astonishment that self-fulfilment is achieved by co-operating with God for good.

Our pilgrimage may reach a daunting place like that described in Mark 8 : 27–37, a place where it requires strong conviction to go forward. It is a cross that has to be borne. To be in the world means being 'well-mingled with the dough' in a phrase of Brother Roger of Taizé.[11] It is tempting to retreat from the world, pass by on the other side, refuse to take risks. Dent challenges us to 'follow the Counsell of David' and be 'up and doing and not to sit still'.[12] Still less to grumble and sit! The risks are often great. In the world's eyes Jesus failed yet it was the work of God. We may too. That is the cross. The Commonwealth of the Puritans failed. On the other hand it brought parliamentary democracy a few important steps nearer. People began criticizing slave-owning in the seventeenth century and the campaign for its abolition went on for generations. In the end its success was sweet to the campaigners, but the emancipated slaves were left desperately poor and still oppressed. Our success may turn out to be as transient as the Sunday School and kindred movements flourishing early in this century and now in serious decline. On God's way in this world there is no escaping the cross at times, though happily most of us do not have to die on it. Whether it is fighting for the environment or trying to protect a child or an animal from abuse, when Christ calls, can his follower in good conscience shut both eyes?

John Wesley's motto is commendable:

> Do all the good you can,
> by all the means you can,
> in all the ways you can,
> in all the places you can,
> at all the times you can,
> to all the people you can,
> as long as ever you can.[13]

*Suggested Exercise – Suggested Encounters*

Read Luke 24 : 13–35, the Road to Emmaus.

In one respect this story is all about endings. Two friends journey, very likely to their home, towards the end of the day; theirs is a road to despair. They have experienced a loss so great that nothing can lift their sadness. Their eyes are fixed to the ground, their hearts are heavy; all hope has flown. Life has become an empty void.

Then a stranger joins them and takes up their weary step. He asks what they were discussing and then hears their sad story. The pain of the past few days comes to the surface.

Suddenly there is a shift of emphasis. It is the turn of the stranger to speak and the two friends are the listeners. As they hear the stranger, recalling the drama of God's redemptive purpose reinterpreted, they are transfixed. The narrative is familiar yet they are grasping it for the first time. Their own story is part of the much greater picture.

But night is falling and they have reached their destination. They press their companion to stay with them and he enters their home. At table he takes the bread and breaks it and they suddenly become aware of who it is that has been with them all along. As the truth dawns and their eyes are opened, he is gone.

They are alone again but no longer as lost souls. Now they are two people who have been re-membered, put back together. They feel charged with energy, their hearts aflame with new hope, their lives transformed by the experience of encounter. All weariness evaporates and they reflect on all they have heard. They get up and go back along the same road but in the opposite direction, back to the future!

- Reflect on the passage.
- Notice the gentle way in which Jesus comes alongside his friends to allow them to speak what was in their hearts.
- Imagine you are on the road and open your heart to the one who waits to hear your story.
- Let your feelings surface as you bring to mind those things which have left you bereft and hurt.
- Note the areas of concern and what comes to light in the conversation.
- Now imagine yourself standing at the door of your home at evening, welcoming this stranger in as a friend.
- Invite him to sit at your table and eat with you – your food.
- Become aware of the growing closeness between the two of you as you recognize that the one who was invited by you now himself invites.
- He breaks bread and offers to share the gift of his own brokenness with you.
- Feel the healing presence of the one who has walked this way before, who is able to lift your burden and set you on a new road.

# 6

# On the Way

## Neighbours and Friends

Life is about learning to love. Day after day we are meeting people, all sorts of people, and most of them we find interesting: neighbours, good and bad. *Pilgrim's Progress* abounds in such encounters. Most of the characters are still around, although they wear different clothes and use a different vocabulary. Moreover, we could add a number of new characters, created by our culture.

Bunyan's purpose, which we endorse, was to warn pilgrims to exercise caution and scrutinize those they met and not to be gullible. It is easy to be charmed by those with a captivating tongue and pleasant manners; a lot of people make it their business to cultivate the art and a great many perform it with excellence. So common a feature of society is this that Bunyan called a whole town Fair-speech after, he said, a noble family of that name.

One of Bunyan's best-known characters is Talkative. In fact, he is not so talkative as Christian, but he is a nuisance to pilgrims because his religion is all talk. While he is 'a Saint abroad' he is 'a Devil at home', as his miserable family knows only too well.[1]

Another fine thumb-nail sketch in *Pilgrim's Progress* is

of By-ends, the arch-hypocrite. He reckons himself a 'Gentleman of good Quality', though everyone knows his great-grandfather worked the river as a waterman, 'looking one way and Rowing another'. And thus the family built up its estates. Furthermore, By-ends married well, into the nobility in fact, his bride being Lord Faining's daughter. He was also proud to have among his ancestors Two-tongues, a cleric. If By-ends has any principle it is never to go against wind or tide. As to church affairs he delights to figure prominently when the sun shines and everyone is smiling and applauding.[2] It is not difficult to match Bunyan's character with some local and national figures.

Hypocrisy is a proven way of rising in the world and Bunyan, like many ordinary folk in every age, despised it and tended to dismiss the whole ruling class of all political colours as guilty of it. His Vanity Town's dignatories are Lords Lechery and Luxury. What angered people was the way a lot of influential people could change sides when the Restoration supplanted the Commonwealth. So Vanity has its Lords Time-server and Turn-about.

We cannot commend Bunyan here, however much we sympathize with his feelings. Allowance has to be made for the pressure temptation exerts on those with power and wealth in society, and today, on those who are stars in the world of entertainment. Moreover, does envy play a part in the judgement of those lower down the social scale? The turncoats have always suffered a bad press but there is evidence to suggest that some of them at least were sincere. They abhorred all revolutions and chose the course they took for the sake of peace and stability. As agents of the Spirit we must try to discern between valid changes of course and those inspired simply by fashion or the desire for gain.

While there were tolerant Calvinists, far too many were prejudiced against those who differed from them. Evangelicals later on took the same line in too many instances. They thought those who failed to respond to the gospel stood condemned as worshippers of false gods, such as pleasure, money, possessions and power. That some people might have serious, reasoned disbeliefs they found hard to concede. Today, if Christians want to be heard, they have to be ready to listen and try to understand ideas very different from their own. Certainly, none of us would think of calling non-believers by the sort of names Bunyan found amusing: Know-nothing, Bats-eyes, Inconsiderate and Light-mind.

The commandment to love your neighbour as yourself (Leviticus 19:18), which Jesus linked with the first commandment, to love God (Luke 10:27f), is something we need to ponder again and again. Like a splendid view from a vantage-point, when seen on different days, at different times and seasons, with glasses to hand, it has always something new and fascinating. Reflecting on experience, prayerfully, leisurely, when whispers seem to emanate from the Spirit, the commandment slowly reveals its magnitude and wonder.

In the Bible itself we see it unfolding until it flowers in Christ. It bursts the narrow limits of Judaism to embrace the whole world. It is the same for the individual. Natural love begins in the home with parental love; it develops into the love of friends and sexual love; it matures, drawn outwards by the commandment, in the love that brings justice, peace and happiness to society.

Our love should imitate God's (Ephesians 5 : 1). It should involve the whole person, reason as well as feeling, action as well as prayer. Brother Roger of Taizé says that if one is going to love others one must be conscious of God's love for us.[3] Unless we know that we are precious to God, are we likely to appreciate the preciousness of those about us?

Luther deepens our understanding of loving in Christ's name. He points out that because Christ has promised to dwell in those who believe in him, we are therefore 'Christs one to another and do to our neighbours as Christ does to us'.[4] Yet to imitate God's love in all its richness is an immense task. His love is compassionate, full of sympathetic understanding, merciful, forgiving, saving; it generates energy and provides help; it is self-denying and infinitely faithful. Yet it is always rigorously holy. Thus, when the Word made flesh went about doing good and challenging the wicked to repent, it led unavoidably to the cross.

One of the strangest verses in the New Testament is 1 Corinthians 13 : 3. 'If I give all I possess to the poor and surrender my body to the flames, but have not love, I gain nothing'. Paul knew Christian martyrs who were devoid of Christian love! How clever we are at self-deceit. It worried Calvin. 'With such blindness,' he says, we love ourselves and

> every man thinketh him selfe to have a just cause
> to advance him selfe, and to despise all other in

comparison of him selfe. If God have given us
any good gift ... we lift up our courage, & not
only swel, but in a maner burst with pride.[5]

Because of this universal tendency the Reformers constantly reminded themselves of their weakness, sinfulness
and mortality. To return to the days when it was fashionable to have one's portrait painted with one hand
caressing the bare dome of a skull is unlikely to appeal
to us, but the symbolism of a cross or a chalice may serve
to jog our memory in the midst of our day-to-day
busyness of our failings and God's grace. It may also
signal us to accept suffering and self-sacrifice, as we are
bidden in Romans 12 : 1, to live in love. But the sacrifice
must be to God and not to win applause.

A friend, according to Dr Johnson, 'is one joined to
another in mutual benevolence and intimacy'.[6] Common
usage, however, dilutes the meaning so that one can
employ the word almost indiscriminately in an endeavour
to be pleasant. The Puritans were well aware of the need
to have friends of the kind meant by Johnson. We often
find pilgrims in pairs on the way; it seems to make the
distance shorter. Christian goes first with Faithful until he
is martyred and then he is found walking with young
Hopeful. Christiana and Mercie are inseparable. Happy
times are conjured up as we read of Baxter and his wife
Margaret often in company with their great friends, John
and Frances Corbet. Today's support groups and counselling sessions, valuable as they are with their expertise,
can never replace tried and trusted friends, ready to share
burdens and secrets, to put themselves out for us as well as

enjoy our entertainment. Why did Jesus send his disciples out two by two? Are we not disciplined and extended by the friend at our side? It has to be remembered, however, that friendship is not as free as it appears. It is costly. It requires vigilance and sacrifice.

Choosing intimate friends, says Bayly, requires care:

> Though thou hast many Acquaintance; yet make not any thy familiar Friend, but he that truly fears God. Such an one thou never need'st to fear. For though you should in some particulars fall out, yet Christian love, the main ground of your friendship, will never fall away.[7]

Although the Reformers had no time for confession – the sacrament of penance – for it gave the priest, they thought, too great a hold over individuals and interposed a person between God and the penitent, they commended people opening their hearts to those they considered able to help them spiritually and keep confidences. Often these would be ministers, but not always; they needed to be friends. Among the Independents and Methodists confessing sins and failings openly to church meetings or classes was strongly encouraged – it was a kind of group therapy – but unless it was skilfully led, it created unhealthy curiosity in some while others indulged in amazing other people with their fertile and sordid imaginings. There was no scriptural pattern for it.

A particular difficulty for many pilgrims is how to relate to those they have to manage. They want to be friendly and helpful but they must not lose their authority or be taken advantage of. *The Larger Catechism*, issued by the Westminster Assembly in 1658, provides some guidelines. Superiors should 'love, pray for, and blesse their inferiors, to instruct, counsel, and admonish them ... providing for them all things necessary for soul and body'.[8] It goes on to point out what hardly needs pointing out, that the sins of those in charge of others are 'an inordinate seeking of themselves, their own glory, ease, profit or pleasure'. It does not mention favouritism, which is an injustice. Actual friendship between superiors and inferiors rather than 'being friendly' is not advisable because of the friction with other employees it inevitably causes.

Today the situation we find ourselves in is one that cries out for a growth in friendship. The security people used to have, living in small communities in large families, seldom leaving home, save to be a servant, a sailor or a soldier, has vanished and in its place we have vast urban developments where people are strangers to one another and we change jobs and move around without putting down deep roots. Loneliness and even suicide have become too common in our depersonalized society. Moreover, modern society has far more elderly people than before, too many of whom feel isolated and neglected.

Full-time ministers are thin on the ground and even with the assistance of non-stipendiaries cannot do the visiting commonly done in former times. Therefore Churches are looking more and more to the laity to make up the short-fall. In the United Reformed Church, as in the Presbyterian Churches from the earliest time, elders are ordained to this work as well as to their duties in church government. The Methodist Church now has pastoral visitors. In the Church of England parishes have their own schemes as Baptist congregations also do in many instances. All are supported by wider-based training programmes. However, the need is so great that no amount of organization can satisfy it. Here is an opportunity for all pilgrims to play a part; it is putting into practice the Priesthood of All Believers and witnessing to the gospel. Perhaps we are beginning to revive the Puritan custom of visiting the poor and the sick, often bearing them gifts, which congregations in those days did on the Sabbath.

## The Sexual Revolution

Were William Shakespeare, Daniel Defoe or Jane Austen to spend a few days with us, they would, of course, be astonished at our computers, televisions and aircraft, but might they not be even more surprised to see the fundamental change that has overtaken relationships between the sexes? The emancipation of women together with the advances made in this century in contraception have brought about a sexual revolution. The ideal of equality between men and women is generally welcomed. It is, after all, only justice. But such a change of attitudes has brought great strain and misery in its wake. The institution of marriage looks dilapidated; countless children are quasi-orphans while the parents are left in a worse state than widows and widowers. The State has the hopeless job of trying to pick up the pieces.

The media constantly harass us with matters to do with sex. It would have seemed very offensive to the Puritans. They were no strangers to sexual misbehaviour and matrimonial squabbling and had plenty to say about such goings-on, but the institution of marriage was not under threat.

Marriage to the Reformers was something dictated by nature herself; they did not see it as sacramental.[9] The sacraments they restricted to the key ones, Baptism and The Lord's Supper. This was to have serious consequences in this century because it meant that divorce was possible where the marriage had broken down irretrievably, broken promises could be forgiven, and remarriage was conceivable, whereas among sacramentalists such a solution to the problem was inconceivable.

That women were held in high esteem in Puritan society seems clear. Indeed, so far as Bunyan is concerned he seems to have a higher opinion of women in general than men. In an age when preachers were not averse to reminding women that Eve, not Adam, was the first sinner, Bunyan goes out of his way to defend the sex. So we find the inn-keeper, Gaius, in *Pilgrim's Progress*, reminding readers that 'God sent forth his Son, made of a Woman', and remarking that no man ever gave Christ 'so much as one Groat', but 'Women followed him, and ministred to him of their Substance'. Moreover, 'Women ... wept when he was going to the Cross' and 'Women (*were*) ... first with him at his Resurrection morn.'[10] Despite all this, Bunyan believed in firmly keeping women in their place, a little below men, and not allowed to preach, pray or speak publicly.

The Reformers warned people to be careful in the choice of a marriage partner. In the language of the time, the *Westminster Confession* says:

> It is lawful for all sorts of people to marry, who are able with judgement to give their consent. Yet it is the duty of Christians to marry only in the Lord, and therefore such as profess the true Reformed religion, should not marry with Infidels, Papists or other Idolaters; neither should such as are godly, be unequally yoked by marrying such as are notoriously wicked in their life, or maintain damnable heresies.[11]

How would we rewrite this for our age? I wonder.

Examining a relationship with judgement, highly regarded by the sober Westminster divines, may seem to us cold and calculating. Yet there are questions which pilgrims should ask themselves before committing themselves. Have we ideals and aims in common? Have we a sufficient degree of tolerance, thoughtfulness for one another to the extent of self-denial, which living under one roof in harmony demands? Do we understand how distinctive Christian love is, being copied from God, with its strong core of faithfulness and its gracious shape?

But what about pilgrims who decide to set off on pilgrimage when they are already wed and their partner does not share their enthusiasm? What is to be done? Christian love is soundly faithful and, despite strains, does its best to sustain the union. In fact, most couples in this situation, and there are many of them, seem to manage contentedly, sharing many values and respecting each other's integrity.

Luther had a happy home. He was incapable of looking after himself. 'Before I married', he confessed, 'the bed was not made up for a whole year and became foul with sweat.'[12] Marriage reformed him! Calvin's story is sad. His only child, a boy, died in infancy, and Idelette, his wife, struggled against illness for a few years and then died. In those days a man was expected to marry again but Calvin refused to and one day in the pulpit he gave his explanation:

> As for me, I do not want anyone to think me very virtuous because I am not married. It would rather be a fault in me if I could serve God better in marriage than remaining as I am ... But I know my infirmity, that perhaps a woman might not be happy with me. However that may be, I abstain from marriage in order that I may be more free to serve God.

T. H. L. Parker wonders what he meant by his infirmity: 'His bad health? Or perhaps his irritability?'[13]

The majority of us get married and the human race continues but not all of us are called to matrimony; after all, Jesus was single.

## Right, Wrong and Reconciliation

In many an ancient parish church as well as in some meeting houses that have survived modernization one can see the Ten Commandments boldly displayed on a wall. It will be the work of the Puritan period. In the Church today hymns, sermons and banners extol God's love for the world *ad infinitum*; there follows the consequence: that we should love one another. In Puritan times it was the sovereignty of the righteous God which was constantly repeated, together with men and women's duty to obey him. So where is the truth? This was the question addressed by P. T. Forsyth, perhaps the most prophetic of all the theologians produced by the Reformed Churches in the British Isles in the last hundred years. Listen to him.

> You hear people say, 'It is a great mistake to be afraid of God. There is nothing to be afraid of. God is love.' But there is everything in the love of God to be afraid of. Love is not holy without judgment. It is the love of holy God that is the consuming fire.[14]

Forsyth was seized by the prominence the holiness of God has in the Scriptures and felt its absence in the Reformed churches of his time. He struggled to restore it to theology and spirituality, but without much success. It is a dimension still missing in our time.

God's holiness is, like the universe, too great for our comprehension, yet in Christ, God reveals something of its mystery, enough for us to ponder and emulate. His holiness combines love and order. In particular, the cross spells out that for us and God to be reconciled, not only is God's love necessary but also his dealing with our wrong-doing and putting us right.

Anyone who seeks to be near to God has to be aware that they are stepping into the holy place. Yes, because God is merciful and gracious he blesses us, deserving and undeserving, answers many prayers and raises us up when we fall, but when we want to know him, live for him, enjoy him, we have to reckon with his holiness. He then calls us to be holy too and this means our love must be holy, flourishing within the framework of morality. All that is wrong in us has to be burnt away. Conscience has to be activated. Our love, like his, can have no truck with evils such as injustice, cruelty, dishonesty, corruption or greed.

Much as we love our companions there are times when we cannot go along with them in their activities and they will be offended. There are times when we have to speak up and not stay silent, risking the wrath of opponents. We may find ourselves ostracized, much against our wishes. But we cannot go to God in the secret place in good conscience unless we have done our best as bearers of Christ's cross. Predicaments like these are happily infrequent for most of us. Moreover, no one with any sense will rush to criticize others; it requires care and prayer; self-examination is essential. We shall often decide to remain silent.

Reproving others is a duty. Obviously parents, teachers, managers and the like must do it but all of us have to tackle it sooner or later. In a sermon on the Cure of Evil Speaking John Wesley says, 'The success of reproof greatly depends on the spirit wherein it is given. Be not therefore wanting in earnest prayer to God, that it may be given in a lowly spirit'.[15] Reprove but never in such a way that people are discouraged and want to give up trying.

We must beware of being judgemental. Sociologists rightly warn us not to be critical if we want to earn the confidence of people such as drug-addicts with deep psychological problems. On the other hand, there are times to express righteous anger, as Jesus himself shows us. How do we learn what to do and when to do it? Our school is at the secret place, before God, where we examine our past conduct and consider how to handle future situations, especially imminent ones, looking to the Lord for the help and guidance he can provide through his Spirit. And how can we go into his presence with any hope of finding comfort and peace if we are deaf to criticism of ourselves? Some criticism, of course, is unjustified or mistaken but a lot contains a germ of truth. Not to heed it is tantamount to dismissing what God is telling us about ourselves.

Holiness has to start in our private lives – what we think and do when we are alone. It is in our private life that temptation finds its most fertile soil.

To know one's own repeated need of forgiveness so as to enter God's presence with confidence and expectancy surely must lead one to nourish a forgiving spirit. Reconciliation and peacemaking are as incumbent upon Christians as extinguishing accidental fires or summoning help if they are too dangerous. Many a disaster has been averted by the alert peacemaker. Without continual forgiveness day after day (Luke 11 : 3–4; 18 : 10–14) the world would, like a machine lacking oil, either grind to a halt or overheat and explode.

You may think you have no enemies and nothing to forgive anybody. In that case you are very fortunate or else you are deluding yourself. A rather more thorough examination of relationships may throw up some surprises. X was one who always opposed you whatever you put forward – it was not a happy relationship. Y was someone against whom you have had a grudge for years. Z pipped you to the post you so wanted; it left a bitter taste. Reconciliation and a clean conscience begin in the forgiving heart.

People are sometimes worried because, although they have forgiven an offender, they cannot forget the offence. We have to accept that we cannot shred memories like unwanted documents; we can, by forgiveness, stop them resurfacing *and* causing distress. As Ecclesiasticus says about not repeating idle gossip, 'let it die with you; be of good courage, it will not burst you' (19 : 10).

'I cannot forgive myself,' we often hear. What spiritual disease has taken root in such a person? A false self-estimate is the problem; a shortage of humility and a surfeit of pride. If God forgives, who am I to refuse to forgive – even if I am the object of the forgiveness?

*Pilgrim's Progress* has a simple story about forgiveness but its poignancy is that Christian, the older pilgrim, leads Hopeful, the younger one, astray. In the allegory they take a short cut over a stile and through a grassy meadow, but it leads to a pit. To their horror they hear another traveller ahead of them crash to his death down the pit and then Christian realizes they have gone astray and that he bears the responsibility for it. Hopeful exclaims that he wishes he had kept to the way he wanted to go and

Christian has no option but to ask his forgiveness: 'I am sorry I have brought thee out of the way, and that I have put thee into such eminent danger; pray, my Brother forgive me, I did not do it of an evil intent.' Hopeful responds gracefully, 'Be comforted my Brother for I forgive thee; and believe too that this shall be for our good.'[16] However, he feels he should take control. 'You shall not go first,' he tells Christian, 'for your mind being troubled, may lead you out of the way again.' What good common-sense! Doubtless Bunyan had some experience of the kind which inspired this tale but what it was we cannot tell. Something similar could happen to any of us.

Their troubles were not over. They escaped the death-trap which consumed their tall fellow-pilgrim called Vain-confidence, but soon found themselves incarcerated in 'a very dark Dungeon, nasty and stinking ... where they lay, from *Wednesday* morning till *Saturday* night, without one bit of bread, or drop of drink, or any light'. Christian 'had double sorrow, because t'was through his inadvised haste that they were brought into this distress'.[17] They were in Doubting Castle in the clutches of Giant Despair.

## Doubt, Despair and Deliverance

Sandy Johnson relates how he once offered to buy a newspaper for Sir Thomas Lipton, the famous grocer/ yachtsman before World War II but the tycoon declined saying that he needed exercise and so Johnson directed him to a shop up the hill. As he disappeared from sight

Johnson remembered that the shop did not sell papers. He spent the rest of Cowes Week keeping out of his way![18] How does anyone feel who has given bad advice to a client or patient? How do you feel if you are chiefly responsible for bringing your company to insolvency or your country to a crisis? But for most of us it is quite bad enough to have led anyone, particularly a young person, astray. We too find that we are in a dark prison.

There are a great many causes of depression. It may be due to some physical trouble. It may be due to the breakdown of marriage, bereavement, an impending court appearance, the collapse of an enterprise, etc. Those who confess the Christian faith may find that they are full of questions about God, his goodness and even his existence. They may feel that their friends are criticizing them behind their backs for lacking genuine faith. It is a consolation, then, to know that Bunyan tells us in *Grace Abounding* of the long time he suffered depression, doubting God's love for him and feeling cast away for ever. Luther suffered bouts of depression. His hyper-activity was followed by exhaustion and pessimism. Happily, many of us do not experience such ups and downs. Like Calvin, we lead busy but steady physical and spiritual lives.

Rightly or wrongly, Bunyan decided that the best way to present doubt and despair to readers was by laughing at them. The method he used was obtained from the old mummers' plays with their slapstick comedy. So we have Giant Despair, armed with his crab-tree cudgel, a brain-less sadist, entirely dependant upon his wife's counsel – plenty of bedroom scenes. Her name is Diffidence which meant in those days one who paralysed others. Upon her instructions the Giant lays about the poor pilgrims, shows them the bones of previous prisoners and leaves them the means of committing suicide.[19]

It is rare to find the discussion of suicide in religious literature and Bunyan is a notable exception. Quite likely he had had to persuade fellow prisoners not to take their lives when things were very bad, with no signs of release and men dying of plague on all sides. The subject is a relevant one for us because of the growing number of suicides, particularly among the young.

Puritan prisoners had all learnt the *Shorter Catechism* and they knew that the sixth commandment forbade, not only killing another unlawfully but, 'the taking away of our own life'. It meant condemnation to hell.[20] On the positive side, they trusted in God's providence. He would end their wretchedness one day. Meanwhile they should 'pluck up the heart of a man'. But Bunyan is realistic enough to have Christian and Hopeful going over the ground more than once. Then, one night, busy in fervent prayer, Christian exclaims how foolish he has been. He has had a key called Promise all the while in his pocket. With this they get out of the dungeon and the castle and, free at last, they return to the stile and the right way. The key was God's promise of salvation.

We have treatments to help us in serious depression. Nevertheless, anyone passing through dark times will find faith in the gospel offering a life-line. Christians have their Good Fridays and their Easter Sundays. As Karl Barth says, 'In faith, man sticks it out with God because he sees that God ... first willed to stick it out with him.'[21]

Jill Jenkin's hymn, 'Living God', enables us to express commitment through hard times in its third verse:

> Lord, when we grow tired of giving,
>  feel frustration, hurt and strain,
> by your Spirit's quiet compulsion,
>  draw us back to you again.
> Guide us through the bitter searching
>  when our confidence is lost;
> give us hope from desolation,
>  arms outstretched upon a cross.[22]

*Suggested Exercise – The Passionate God*

Read Mark 12:28–34.

Reflect on the simplicity of Jesus' answer. For him all human affairs are summed up in the broad sweep of the central tenets of the Mosaic Law.

> *Hear, O Israel, the Lord our God, the Lord is one. Love the Lord your God with all your heart and with all your soul and with all your mind and with all your strength. The second is this, Love your neighbour as yourself.* (vv. 29–31.)

Four words jump out at us from this text: heart, soul, mind and strength. It is an image of wholeness and totality. There is wholeness and totality in God; it is revealed in Jesus – through his birth, life, words and sacrifice. And we are called to return the love first shown us, honouring his name and following his ways.

We are the apple of his eye (Deuteronomy 32 : 10) and he is passionate about us. How do we respond to this? Do we truly believe this?

The following is an extract taken from material produced for the Portsmouth Diocese 1997 Lent Course by the Revd Dr Philip Newell:

> What is of value in life that happens without passion? If we do not feel passionate about one another, or about what it is that we are doing or studying or creating together, what will happen? Surely it is no coincidence that the gift of passion between a man and woman is what gives rise to conception and life. Similarly the passion that exists in an artist, the passion of a mother for her child, or the passion in a people to be freed from oppression, and all the day to day passions of interest in work and play and relationships are what give rise to creativity and new beginnings in our lives. What are the passions of faith and hope, and above all, what are the passions of love that are to be rediscovered in our lives and in the church and world?

And further:

> The Gospel is given not primarily to tell us that many of our passions are dark and destructive, for we more or less know that about ourselves

and about all people. The truth which we have forgotten and which the Gospel is given to recall us to, and thus to liberate us with, is that we bear within ourselves the passion and the creativity of God. Grace is given to release those creative desires from our very depths and to free us from the powers of lethargy and destructiveness that obscure what is truest in us as God's sons and daughters.[23]

Read Psalm 139 : 1–18, 23f.

Embrace your own being for it is known through and through.

# 7

# Today and Tomorrow

## On Course

'Passengers, please fasten your seat-belts. We are entering an area of turbulence.' An announcement familiar to air-travellers. Sudden ups and downs are to be anticipated. Happily, the aircraft's engines keep going regardless. At last the trouble is cleared and we cruise quietly along in a deep blue sky. The rhythm of spiritual life with God beats steadily whatever mood or tempo events bring about.

All spiritual traditions insist on maintaining that rhythm. The Puritans had their own way of putting it. However tired, frustrated, disgruntled or excited we may feel, 'the least we can doe is call upon him [the Lord] constantly morning and evening', says Preston.[1] If we have committed ourselves to God's service, we should wait upon him 'as a servant waits on his master, ready to observe his will, and do his work'. As his children and friends we should cast all our cares upon him. But we are not only servants and children, we are priests, going to and fro between two worlds and it is our business to be 'in God's house', the secret place, every day, as well as in the world, for we need 'mercy from him' and we 'have work to do for him'.[2] The engines keep going regardless.

After the wretchedness of incarceration in Doubting Castle, Christian and Hopeful are astounded to find themselves among the Delectable Mountains, which Bunyan describes as though he were a travel-agent preparing a brochure on holidays in the Tyrol. Christian and Hopeful, by now inured to trial and trouble, have forgotten what it is to smile and enjoy themselves. They fear lest they have strayed once again. 'Is this the way?' they inquire of some shepherds, who assure them that it is.[3]

There are surely more happy than woeful days in life. Yet it is surprising how often Christians are doubtful about enjoying life and may feel guilty about it. They seem tarred with the ancient pagan brush of the Greeks who felt doom impending whenever things went well because the gods were sure to get jealous. Is our God at all like that?

It is much to the credit of the divines who met at Westminster that when they published *The Larger Catechism* in 1658 the first question and answer read:

> What is the chief and highest end of man?
> Man's Chief and Highest End is to glorify God, and fully to enjoy him for ever.[4]

It sounds like living in the spirit of Handel's 'Hallelujah Chorus'! However, it implies something more than exultation: a deep and lasting satisfaction with God and his designs.

How is it, then, that folklore has invariably associated religion with gravity and dullness, while those who want to enjoy themselves go their way carefree and full of fun?

This is, of course, caricature, yet it has a point. Mark Rutherford (alias William Hale-White) was perhaps soured by his sad experience as a theological student and a young minister in a Congregational church in the middle of the nineteenth century but he unwittingly points to the source of the caricature. In his *Auto-biography* he shows what happens when Reformed, Evangelical religion loses its spiritual vitality. He was disgusted at the narrowmindedness of fellow-students whose conversation was all about chapel goings-on and whose ambitions were to win wealthy pulpits and marry themselves off well. Church members he found came to worship out of custom and preachers were expected to reiterate the 'old story' for the comfort of their hearers but never to stir their minds. What he observed was that 'the old deity once alive' had 'hardened into an idol'.[5] Correct doctrine alone is no more use than a fine new road if no one makes use of it. When the practice of the Christian faith has fallen to such a low level, how can it be other than dull and joyless? All it can do is contribute to what folklore has always said.

The best of Puritan preachers and writers enjoin Christians to enjoy all that God gives them and to give him thanks. They should not dwell on the past. It is no use to God and makes reconciliation defective if people will keep on going over past sins and thus rendering them-selves not only joyless but unfruitful. Baxter sums it up:

> O the sinful folly of many of the saints, who drench their spirits in continual sadness, and waste their days in complaints and groans, and

> ... so make themselves, both in body and mind
> unfit for this sweet and heavenly work! (*i.e.
> church worship*) When they should join with
> the people of God in his praises, and delight
> their souls in singing to his name, they are
> questioning their worthiness, and studying their
> miseries, or raising scruples ... (*They*) rob God
> of his praise and themselves of their solace.[6]

Nor is it enough to enjoy praising God in worship; if we look for it, there is so much to enjoy, so much to care about. Living with the blinds drawn, introspectively, as too many people do, only stimulates anxiety and prostration. Pull up the blinds, look outwards: that is the way to joy and peace (cf. Phil. 4 : 4–9).

Christian and Hopeful begin enjoying their holiday. They go sightseeing and they walk on the mountains. One day they climb one called Clear. On the top there is a telescope for visitors to use and it is provided free by the shepherds! No ordinary shepherds these. 'If they have skill,' they are told, 'they might see the Gates of the Cœlestial City.' Not being very familiar with such instruments, they fail to focus well, yet 'they thought they saw something like the Gate, and some of the glory of the place'. And so they went on their way singing.[7]

'Christians today do not often think of heaven, rarely hear sermons on heaven, and would regard it as totally unreal if they were expected to say that they long for heaven.' This was Nathaniel Micklem's view nearly sixty years ago. Is it not still true? 'Heaven is unreal.' Micklem was perhaps the leading theologian among Congregationalists, a true son of the Reformation, and Principal of Mansfield College, Oxford. He roundly attributed this attitude to 'religious shallowness'. The cross of Christ is emptied of its meaning if life beyond death is unreal. The goal of all his striving and ours is reduced to a fantasy.[8] We are like actors who rehearse their play but never stage it. Spiritual life never reaches its consummation.

While the Christian emphasis has always been on knowing God through Christ here and now and looking forward to seeing him 'face to face' hereafter – the foremost joy – this is not to say that the society of heaven is of no importance. When the Puritans spoke of the Eternal City they were not only reflecting Revelation 21 but inferring that heaven is the place of fellowship and activity. But it is also the place of healing and wiping away tears. It is no place for evil. Its citizens are those not only raised to new life but sorted out in judgement. When we gather at the Lord's Supper all these things are foreshadowed: judgement and healing, communion with God in Christ and with one another, including those who have gone before us, 'the saints'.

## Quiescence or Resurgence

Before leaving the shepherds Christian and Hopeful were warned about 'the Inchanted Ground they would have to cross; they were bidden not to be tempted to go to sleep.'[9] However, when they reached there, the air was heavy and Hopeful wearily suggested taking a nap to refresh them. Christian deterred him and he had to acknowledge that two heads were better than one. By one means and another they manage to keep alert.[10] Many of us are to be discovered resting, nodding.

In all parts of life, physical and spiritual, there comes a period when knowledge and experience induce a sense of self-assurance and security, tinged with pride, which observers perceive to be complacency. It happens to individuals and institutions and the Church provides plenty of examples of it. Resistance to change and conservatism characterize it but time is always moving on and forcing change, even if only in the shape of decay. As athletes who rest too long lose their fitness so do complacent Christians become flabby, with conscience blunt, witness extinguished and love grown cold. Temptation seizes the opportunity offered and some Christians slip into the clutches of sensuality while others stray into the service of Mammon; churches fall to quarrelling or are sucked into money-raising as their life-mission. Meanwhile, to survive, spirituality has to go underground.

One of the stories concerning the hermits who lived in the Egyptian deserts in the fourth century is about two monks, Joseph and Lot, a senior man who seems to have acted as father-confessor to the other. Joseph told Lot how, to the best of his ability – he was a modest fellow – he kept his little rule: prayer, fasting, meditation and quiet. What more could he do? Abbot Lot rose up and extended his hands towards the heavens. His fingers became like torches of fire and he cried, 'If thou wilt thou shalt be made wholly flame.'[11] When spirituality becomes a daily drill and the longing to do better has vanished, a crisis is round the corner: either reform or wither away.

Like a house or a business, there is constant need for repair and improvement in the spiritual life, for individuals, churches and denominations. Failure only leads to tragedy.

In our day, while hermits are rare and entrants into religious orders are on the decline, it is curious that there are people who think they can pursue Christian spirituality on their own, without being involved in church and congregational life. No one in the New Testament belonged to this school of thought. Isolation cannot help the cause of reform. The Church's teaching and practice needs the newcomer's insights.

Karl Barth used to say that the ignorance of God in the world was very disturbing but the ignorance of God in the Church was even more serious. For example, God as love is perpetually proclaimed, with acclamations of joy, Sunday by Sunday, but who speaks of God's righteousness? Not many. Who speaks of God's holiness? How many banners are made depicting the broad and narrow ways? God's will is for the salvation of the world; it is a serious and painful business.

But what are the criteria for reform? These the Reformers found, as we all know, in the Bible. 'The Holy Scriptures of the old and new Testaments are the Word of God, the only rule of Faith and Obedience,' says *The Larger Catechism*.[12] This points us up the stairway to reform but does not take us to the top. How is what we find in the Bible to be made relevant for today? Congregations are repeatedly told that what is needed is the help and inspiration of the Holy Spirit. Can we explain what this means? Perhaps a comparison with art may help, for God has made us creative like artists. They train in schools and by visiting art-galleries and eventually produce their own work, some more original than others. Christians learn their lessons in the school and galleries of the Bible and then go on to produce their own work, some more valuable than others. For reform to germinate it requires a good grounding in the Bible together with the help, guidance and inspiration God gives through his Spirit, a process which arises from a prayerful life. But unless the particular reform is simply for an individual, for it to grow and succeed it must strike a chord with other Christians. Too many churchgoers are like Lot's wife, backward-looking.

Reform and change in recent times have transformed many Reformed churches' worship. In turn this affects private devotion. Take symbolism for instance. While symbolism is inescapable in communicating with the public – inn-signs and coats of arms illustrate this – Reformed churches were highly critical of their use in worship. They were reacting against the medieval, often superstitious, use of them. But symbolism was bound to come back and when the Edinburgh printer, George Mossman, produced *The Principal Acts of the General Assembly* of the Church of Scotland in 1691, he felt the need of a logo. His brainwave was the burning bush with the words, *nec tamen consumebatur* (and yet it was not consumed) and this proved popular down the centuries, both on Presbyterian publications and eventually in churches on pulpit-falls and in stained-glass windows. The Word of God never dies. It consumes but goes on burning. However, as Exodus 3:3 shows: there has to be somebody who will turn aside and observe it carefully![13]

The twentieth century has witnessed how some biblical verses can bear prodigious fruit. John 17 : 20–23 has inspired the Ecumenical Movement which has transformed the face of the Christian Church at all levels, in towns, countries and on the world scene. The words make plain that the will of Christ is Christian unity. It was but a dearly loved dream to Baxter and Bunyan and their generation. They did not want separation but were obliged to accept it. The Reformed Churches have played a leading part in ecumenism, as also their missionary bodies. There are innumerable ecumenical projects of different kinds but not so much physical union between denominations save for the notable instance of the Congregationalists and Presbyterians to form The United Reformed Church in 1972.

What we find today is that local congregations, whatever their brand of Protestantism may be, will probably have people who have grown up and spent much of their lives in a different denomination and are happy enough in their new home. On all sides barriers between Christians are falling down. There are opportunites galore for keen Christians to share with people of traditions different from their own: worship and prayer, study, socializing, common projects, all contribute. Though our differences are not removed – some may be – what is refreshing and reassuring is the discovery that we share more on our spiritual journey than ever we thought. All of us must keep pressing up this road of reform.

Another exploration is now in our sights. If ecumenicity, toleration and the quest for truth have any meaning for us, we may well feel a call to sit down with our fellow-beings who belong to other faiths. In the past this was frowned upon, if not forbidden. It smacked of dallying with false gods. Now we know that we are living in a very small planet, where communication between places thousands of miles apart is instantaneous, and where we must learn to respect one another and make peace work. That God, who obviously loves diversity and has made many races and cultures, also has variations in the manner of the spiritual life is not surprising. Indeed Christians can learn much from those experienced in other traditions. There is nothing to fear. If we only speak the truth as we know it, then Christ himself, through the Spirit, is the advocate for the faith. But we have to listen or we miss opportunities and miss targets. Any sense of superiority or spirit of rivalry has to be dismissed at once; they are incompatible with loving your neighbour.

## Growing Shorter and Taller

Least convincing is the concluding phase of *Pilgrim's Progress*, their sojourn in the Country of Beulah before crossing the river to the City of Zion. 'In this place they met with abundance of what they had sought for in their Pilgrimage.' All is bliss. The pilgrims enjoy strolling about amongst orchards, vineyards and gardens and they love to snooze in the pleasant arbours.[14] It is not what we observe today of old age. However, it has to be remembered that in the seventeenth century the geriatric problem had not arrived. Nevertheless, we find John Owen lamenting his situation as he stepped into Beulah's fair land. Writing to a friend he assures him that he continues in the Lord's work 'according to my weak measure'. He wants to be ready when death comes. 'I have daily warnings from my age', he says, 'and many infirmities.' Life expectancy was not high in those days. He was at the time fifty-four and was to live well over ten more years![15]

Retirement is still often presented in blissful terms and indeed, having thrown off the burdens and chains of business or employment, people certainly have unprecedented freedom to fill their hours and days as they please. At last there is time for couples to share activities and interests as never before. There are opportunities to get to know the grandchildren or the 'adopted grandchildren'. Games and hobbies provide hours of pleasure and lead to new friendships. There is bliss.

The choice, however, hides a spiritual question. What shall we do with our talents, experience and energies? Can a devoted disciple of Jesus Christ, who is often in the secret place of prayer, decide not to take up any responsibilities in church or community life because they want to be free to do as they like? Such a wide variety of voluntary work exists, all crying out for helpers. Once involved, it is astonishing and pleasing to find how well represented churches are in the field.

Old age, then, is like Beethoven's Mass in D. It has beauty and moments of sublimity, yet it reflects tremendous spiritual conflict, roughness, not just calm.

Everyone knows how prone the elderly are to reminisce. Young people may be enthralled or bored stiff, while contemporaries become used to repeatedly hearing beloved tales. But the serious side is when younger people seek the wisdom of older ones. What do they advise? What has been their experience? What would they do? It is humbling because the old owl is only too aware of the frailty and unreliability of the advice that comes to mind but it may serve to encourage someone who is puzzled about what to do. Experience may play a part in inducing them to act with patience, tolerance and prudence.

Looking back over one's life and times there is bound to be regret. Wars hot and wars cold are not happy times. There is probably not very much to be proud of. Nevertheless, the feeling of pilgrims and many others is one of gratitude. What happy memories photographs revive. Once I took a funeral for a woman who had been an agnostic and so was the widower. I had to explain to him that I only conducted funerals in the Christian liturgy, at which he smiled amicably and said, 'You do that. As for me, I just want to say thanks for her and everything, but I don't know if there's anyone to thank.' Christians would praise God for his providence.

The old Calvinist doctrine of Predestination has few supporters nowadays and yet when we survey the past, what we have done, where we came to crossroads and turned this way or that, it may well seem that, if not predestined, we have been guided and blessed. W. R. Matthews, long the Dean of St Pauls and no mean philosopher, in his autobiography, *Memories and Meanings*, with the modesty that was typical of him, says how diffident he felt about claiming that providence had taken control of events in his life. It sounded arrogant to say this, 'as if we presumed to claim to be favourites of God'. 'Yet', he feels obliged to say, 'some turning points were so decisive and opened up such unforseen opportunities that we do feel bound to take them as due to the grace of God.'[16]

Pilgrims will probably also recall certain times when God has seemed unusually close to them, perhaps giving them peace in the midst of turmoil or restraining them from foolish action, giving them a precious insight they needed or strength to accomplish something they felt was beyond them: further reasons for gratitude. Sibbes said they were drops of heaven God gave us for our encouragement.[17]

Though the pilgrim's faith in the God of Salvation is now strong and doubts have been dismissed, there remain perplexities.

The problem of suffering is never far away. I can recall the ghostly figures who emerged from Belsen when Germany was invaded. Who can forget the sad antics and cries of mentally-sick patients locked out of sight of the world, if one has seen and heard them? And what of friends or loved ones who face constant pain and weakness? In praying about these tragic people one has to remember God who has taken upon himself the role of the suffering servant. Why suffering, why crucifixion, hold the key to the salvation of the world is a well-hidden secret. Yet it has to be said that suffering evokes tremendous compassion and sacrifice and this seems necessary to balance the human will to be selfish, grasping, unjust, ruthless, in a word, sinful. The story of the Fall in Genesis 3 suggests that suffering is the price of sin.

What we know is that it is excruciating. We are reluctant to accept that the way to salvation, to holiness and peace, takes us through fire, for 'our God is a consuming fire' (Hebrews 12 : 29).

All present-day pilgrims surely have the future of the planet in their prayers. After all, we plead with the Creator and one who has a long and distinguished career as a Saviour. It is hardly possible to walk in the country, travel or shop in a market without remembering that we need something more than human endeavour for the earth to survive, and that we depend on God. But it is not the only subject for concern. There are many others, of course, but one which should exercise us more than it does is the present technological/economic system which is producing injustice, greed and waste as well as unemployment and misery. How will this end? Will it collapse and bring down our civilization like others before it? Or will providence decide otherwise? And is there something we should be doing?

So the pilgrims draw near to the river. Some are fearful, others not. Preaching at the funeral of Mary Charlton, Baxter spoke to those who were fearful. He asked them how they receive friends after a long and dangerous journey or after 'some bloody fight?' He did not answer his question but left the congregation to do so and then he reminded them that the Saviour had 'a larger heart'.[18]

Poor Christian: 'great horror' fell upon him. 'He in great measure lost his senses, so that he could neither remember nor orderly talk.' The sins of his youth troubled him again and apparitions of Hobgoblins pursued him before eventually in peace he passed over. Hopeful had an easy passage and Christiana too.[19]

In his dream Bunyan hears the Bells of heaven ring out for the pilgrims, which is a wonderfully strange thing, seeing that bell-ringing was sinful in the Puritan way of thinking. True spirituality overcomes sectarian and narrow-minded religion.

> Who would true Valour see
> Let him come hither;
> One here will constant be,
> Come Wind, come Weather.
> There's no Discouragement
> Shall make him once Relent,
> His first avow'd Intent,
> To be a Pilgrim.[20]

*Suggested Exercise – Coming Full Circle*

Read Deuteronomy 30:11–16; 19f.

Moses delivers this inspiring speech to the children of Israel just before they cross the Jordan. He is an old man and knows he will soon die. The vision of the Promised Land that sustained his people through their long wanderings is soon to become a reality. But he is not to be part of it; his task is over and he must let go. The people have to continue without him on their journey to freedom. Just before he hands over to Joshua he addresses the people from his heart. He exhorts them to 'choose life' and own their God. In this manner and along this road they will find the fulfilment of promise.

The journeying motif is strongly etched throughout Scripture and we need to remind ourselves over and over again that in these stories of patriarchs and prophets, as well as those of the exodus and exile, God's will was always discerned *en-route* to a new venture. Nor should we forget that the first Christians were known as people of the Way.

It should not surprise us, then, that Bunyan, steeped in all the resonances of pilgrimage, should choose to re-inforce this idea of passage. By placing his protagonist, Christian, on a long and difficult road he is seeking to draw parallels between his own narrative and the great journeying theme of the Bible.

Look at the picture of the Celtic Knot.

Notice how the pattern of strands are woven in and around each other, creating an intricate design.

With a coloured pencil or pen take one strand at a time and colour it in, following its meandering path round the circle.

- What do you see emerging?
- What do you experience as you travel along this road?
- Where do you finish?
- Has this anything to say to you?

'The end is where we start from.'[21]

# Appendix 1

# A Note on the Text of
# The Pilgrim's Progress

Bunyan's *The Pilgrim's Progress* has been reprinted in countless editions over the centuries. Those of the last century were usually amended to conform with current taste – a tinker's hot words needed cooling down at times. In 1960 Professor Roger Sharrock published through the Oxford University Press the definitive text of Bunyan's masterpiece, based on the earliest editions. In this book my quotations from *The Pilgrim's Progress* are taken from N. H. Keeble's *John Bunyan: The Pilgrim's Progress*, OUP, 1984. It has the seventeenth century flavour about it, whereas Roger Sharrock's edition, Penguin, 1965, with the same title, loses it, its spelling and general presentation having been modernized.

In the notes to the chapters I refer to both editions: e.g. OUP p. 10; Peng. p. 11.

# Appendix 2

# Brief Notes on the English Reformers Quoted

AMBROSE, Isaac (1604–62/3)
Much esteemed in his time for his spirituality, then called piety. Spent every May in retreat in woods at Hoghton Tower, near Blackburn. Ministered at Preston and later Garstang. Ejected 1662. His outspokenness caused imprisonment more than once. Left few writings.

BAXTER, Richard (1615–91)
Minister at Kidderminster; became a model for Dissenters. Parliamentary chaplain to army. At Restoration lost his living; was offered bishopric but refused; suffered fines and imprisonment. Prominent theologian and ethical writer; wrote some hymns, e.g. 'Ye holy angels bright.' Worked for toleration and ecumenism.

BAYLY, Lewis (d. 1631)
Bishop of Bangor (1616). In trouble for accusing Privy Councillors of popery and for condemning the Book of Sports and suffered imprisonment. Had popular appeal as writer.

DOWNAME, John (d. 1652)

Rector of All Hallows-the-Great, London and Tuesday Lecturer at St Bartholomew's. Campaigned for the poor.

EDWARDS, Jonathan (1703–50)

Minister at Northampton (America) (1727–50). Came to hold narrow views of membership – extreme Congregationalism – and was forced to resign. A pioneer in mission to the Indians. Theologian of revivalism; rigid Calvinist yet something of a mystic. Appointed President of Princeton but died very soon afterwards.

GOODWIN, Thomas (1600–80)

Chaplain to the Council of State (1649); President of Magdalen College, Oxford (1650); prominent at the Westminster Assembly. Removed at Restoration; formed an Independent congregation in London. Tolerant Calvinist and leading Independent. Wrote on church government and other subjects.

HENRY, Matthew (1662–1714)

Minister of large Presbyterian congregation at Chester; moved to Hackney (1712). Chiefly remembered for his Bible commentary, published in five volumes (1708–10) and often reprinted and re-edited since.

NORTON, Thomas (1532–84)

Lawyer and Member of Parliament. Also poet and playwright. Translated Calvin's *Institutes* soon after publication. Bishop of London's solicitor and 'censor' of literature. Had a grim reputation for torturing Roman Catholics.

OWEN, John (1616–83)
Minister in Essex; became a chaplain to Cromwell; then Dean of Christ Church, Oxford and Vice Chancellor of the University of Oxford. At the Restoration he gathered a congregation in London. Pre-eminent as Calvinist theologian; Congregationalist. After the Fire of London distributed a thousand guineas for Charles II to the poor of the city.

PERKINS, William (1518–1602)
Famous preacher at Great St Andrew's, Cambridge; also teacher and writer. He aimed to show Christian theology as the 'science of living blessedly for ever'.

PRESTON, John (1587–1628)
Dean of Queen's College, Cambridge; later preacher at Lincoln's Inn, London. Chaplain to Charles I and used often as a political agent.

SIBBES, Richard (1577–1635)
Lost his Cambridge University posts for his Puritanism (1615); became preacher at Gray's Inn, London (1617). Later was Master of St Catherine's Hall, Cambridge and then went to Holy Trinity in the city. Good administrator yet also well known for his spirituality. Issac Walton said that 'heaven was in him before he was in heaven'.

# Suggestions for Further Reading

Bell, John, *States of Bliss and Yearning*, Iona, 1998.

Foster, Richard, *Prayer – The Heart's True Home*, Hodder and Stoughton, 1992.

Forsyth, P. T., *The Soul of Prayer*, reprinted by Paternoster Press, 1998.

McGrath, Alister E., *Beyond the Quiet Time*, SPCK, 1995.

Marty, Martin and Micah, *When True Simplicity is Gained – Finding Spiritual Clarity in a Complex World*, Eerdman's Publishing Co., 1998.

Packer, James I., *Among God's Giants: Aspects of Puritan Christianity*, Kingsway, 1991.

McGrath, Alister E., *Roots that Refresh – a Celebration of Reformation Spirituality*, Hodder and Stoughton, 1991.

Furlong, Monica, *Puritan's Progress – a Study of John Bunyan*, Hodder and Stoughton, 1975.

Parker, T. H. L., *John Calvin: A Biography*, J. M. Dent & Sons, 1975.

Nuttall, Geoffrey F., *Richard Baxter*, Nelson, 1965.

# Notes

(The place of publication is London unless otherwise stated.)

## 1 Then and Now

1. T. S. Eliot, 'Little Gidding', p. 197, *The Complete Poems and Plays*, Faber and Faber, 1969.
2. Alister McGrath, *Roots that Refresh*, Hodder and Stoughton, 1991, pp. 20f.
3. Gordon Rupp, *The Righteousness of God*, Hodder and Stoughton, 1953, p. 118.
4. Albert Peel, *The Congregational Two Hundred*, Independent Press, 1948, p. 39.
5. R. S. Thomas, *Collected Poems, 1945–1990*, Phoenix Division, Orion, 1993.

## 2 Making a Start

1. OUP pp. 8, 145ff. Peng. p. 11, 157ff. (See Appendix 1)
2. Jim Thompson, *Stepney Calling*, Mowbray, 1991, p. 3.
3. Richard Baxter, *The Saint's Everlasting Rest*, *Works* (Orme), 1830, vol. XXIII, p. 341.
4. Arthur Dent, *The Plaine-man's Pathway to Heaven*, 1601, pp. 204f.
5. T. S. Eliot, *The Waste Land* V. line 329, *The Complete Poems and Plays*, Faber, 1961.
6. John Preston, *The Deformed Forme of a Formal Profession*, n.d.

7. Christopher Hill, *The World Turned Upside Down*, Temple Smith, 1972, p. 139.
8. K. Lawson, *Spirituality – Forming and Reforming*, Edinburgh, 1995 (see Acknowledgements), p. 4.
9. OUP p. 9. Peng. p. 12.
10. OUP pp. 15ff. Peng. pp. 18ff.
11. Richard Sibbes, *Works*, Nichol, 1864, I, p. 142.
12. OUP pp. 17, 20. Peng. pp. 21, 24.
13. Geoffrey F. Nuttall, *Richard Baxter*, Nelson, 1965, p. 9.
14. Jonathan Edwards, *Life of the Revd David Brainerd*, Glasgow, 1829, p. 57.
15. OUP pp. 8f. Peng. pp. 11f.
16. Sibbes, *Works* I, Orwell, cxxvi.
17. Baxter, *Everlasting Rest*, *Works*, Orme, 1830, vol. XXIII, p. 307.
18. OUP p. 23. Peng. p. 27.
19. OUP p. 156. Peng. p. 169.
20. J. G. Whittier, 'Dear Lord and Father of mankind,' verse 5. A hymn to be found in many hymn-books.

### 3  Getting a Grounding

1. Matthew Henry, *The Sabbath*, Nelson, 1847, p. 281.
2. Jonathan Edwards, *Treatise Concerning Religious Affections*, 1746, p. 28.
3. John Owen, *The Lord's Supper*, 1674, Discourse X. II.
4. OUP p. 236. Peng. p. 252.
5. John Owen, *Rules for Christian Fellowship* (pamphlet), n.d. Sect. 7.
6. OUP p. 24. Peng. p. 28.
7. Richard Baxter, *Gildas Silvianus: the Reformed Pastor* (1656), *Works* (Orme), 1830, vol. XVI, p. 281.
8. Richard Sibbes, *The Soul's Conflict with Itself*, *Works*, Edinburgh, Grossard, 1862, I. p. 193.
9. Isaac Ambrose, *Looking unto Jesus*, Edinburgh, 1723, p. 384.

10. Michael O'Mara, *On a Clear Day*, 1995, p. 76.
11. John Preston, *A Preparation for the Lord's Supper*, London, n.d., p. 94.
12. Jonathan Edwards, *Treatise Concerning Religious Affections* 1746, p. 33.
13. OUP p. 31. Peng. p. 35f.
14. John Calvin, *Institutes*, Tr. Thomas Norton, 1678 edn, 4.1.21.

4   *In Touch with God*

1. OUP p. 45. Peng. p. 49.
2. Richard Baxter, Funeral Sermon for Mary Charlton, 1672.
3. William Perkins, *A Graine of Musterd-Seede*, *Works*, 1626, p. 643.
4. Lewis Bayly, *The Practice of Piety*, 1699 edn, p. 161.
5. Calvin, *Institutes*, 2.20.6.
6. *Ibid*. 3.20.8.
7. *Ibid*. 3.7.4.
8. *Ibid*. 3.20.12.
9. Gordon Rupp, *The Righteousness of God*, Hodder and Stoughton, 1953, p. 316.
10. Calvin, *Institutes*, 3.20.38.
11. Kenneth Lawson, *Spirituality – Forming and Reforming*, Edinburgh, 1995 (see Acknowledgements), p. 33.
12. A. G. Dickens, *The English Reformation*, B. T. Batsford, 1964, p. 55.
13. Richard Baxter, *The Saint's Everlasting Rest*, *Works* (Orme), 1830, vol. XXIII, p. 3.
14. Matthew Henry, *Directions for Daily Communion with God*, 1712, pp. 43, 62.
15. Dag Hammarskjöld, *Markings*, Faber and Faber, 1964, p. 23.
16. Baxter, *Everlasting Rest*, vol. XXIII, p. 303.
17. Henry, *Directions*, pp. 68–76.

18. *A Book of Services and Prayers*, The Congregational Church in England and Wales, 1959, pp. 278f.
19. OUP pp. 46, 50ff., 199ff. Peng. pp. 51, 55ff., 214ff.
20. Bayly, *Practice*, p. 200.
21. Thomas Goodwin, *A Childe of Light Walking in Darkness*, 1643, p. 29.
22. Richard Sibbes, *Divine Meditations*, *Works*, 1864 edn, VII, p. 203.
23. OUP p. 197. Peng. p. 212.
24. OUP pp. 46ff. Peng. pp. 51ff.
25. Jim Thompson, *Stepney Calling*, Mowbray, 1991, p. 106.
26. OUP p. 197. Peng. p. 212.
27. OUP pp. 51f. Peng. pp. 56ff.
28. OUP p. 200. Peng. p. 215.
29. Goodwin, *A Childe of Light*, pp. 153, 156, 140.

5   *In the World*

1. OUP pp. 79, 231. Peng. pp. 85, 247.
2. Matthew Henry, *Directions for Daily Communion with God*, 1712, p. 59.
3. Matthew Arnold, *Culture and Anarchy*, 1869.
4. OUP p. 138. Peng. p. 150.
5. Richard Baxter, *The Saint's Everlasting Rest*, *Works* (Orme), 1830, XXIII p. 10.
6. John Downame, *A Guide to Godlynesse*, 1629, p. 264.
7. OUP p. 195. Peng. p. 210.
8. Richard Baxter, *A Christian Directory*, 1673, II.xvii.
9. OUP p. 231. Peng. p. 347.
10. Lord Chesterfield, *Letters*, 1774, Dent, 1984, p. 308.
11. Rex Brico, *Taizé*, Collins, 1978, p. 172.
12. Arthur Dent, *The Plaine Man's Path-way to Heaven*, 1601, p. 371.
13. George Eayrs (ed.), *Letters of John Wesley*, Hodder and Stoughton, 1915, p. 423.

6   *On the Way*

1. OUP p. 64. Peng. p. 70.
2. OUP p. 81. Peng. p. 87.
3. Rex Brico, *Taizé*, Collins, 1978, p. 155.
4. Martin Luther, *Works*, Philadelphia, 1943, quoted by Gordon Rupp, *The Righteousness of God*, Hodder and Stoughton, 1953, p. 232.
5. John Calvin, *Institutes*, 3.7.4.
6. *Shorter Oxford English Dictionary*, 3rd edn, Oxford, Clarendon Press, 1944, p. 752.
7. Lewis Bayly, *The Practice of Piety*, 1699, p. 164.
8. *The Larger Catechism*, 1658, L3.
9. *Westminster Confession*, 1648, XXIV, XXVIII.
10. OUP p. 217. Peng. pp. 232f.
11. *Westminster Confession*, XXIV.III.
12. Rupp, *Righteousness*, p. 351.
13. T. H. L. Parker, *John Calvin*, Dent, 1975, p. 102.
14. P. T. Forsyth, *The Work of Christ*, Hodder and Stoughton, 1910, reprinted by Independent Press, 1946, p. 95.
15. John Wesley, *Standard Sermons*, ed. E. H. Sugden, Epworth, 1921, XLII.
16. OUP p. 92. Peng. p. 99.
17. OUP p. 93. Peng. p. 100
18. Air Vice-Marshall Sandy Jordan, *Diary of an Aviator*, Airlife, Shrewsbury, 1993, p. 5.
19. OUP pp. 93ff. Peng. pp. 100ff.
20. *Shorter Catechism*, A a 2.
21. Karl Barth, *The Christian Life*, Edinburgh, T & T Clark 1981. p. 282.
22. *Rejoice and Sing*, Oxford, Oxford University Press, Hymn 530.
23. Philip Newell, *The Pilgrimage of Return*, (see Acknowledgements).

7 *Today and Tomorrow*

1. John Preston, *The Saint's Daily Exercise*, n.d., p. 17.
2. Matthew Henry, *Directions for Daily Communion with God*, 1712, p. 48.
3. OUP pp. 97f. Peng. p. 104.
4. *The Larger Catechism*, A1.
5. Mark Rutherford, *Autobiography*, Hodder and Stoughton, n.d., pp. 42, 53, 46.
6. Richard Baxter, *The Saint's Everlasting Rest*, *Works* (Orme), 1830, vol. XXIII, p. 304.
7. OUP p. 100. Peng. p. 107.
8. Nathaniel Micklem, *The Creed of a Christian*, SCM Press, 1940, p. 163.
9. OUP pp. 111f. Peng. pp. 118f.
10. OUP p. 112. Peng. p. 119.
11. Helen Waddell, *The Desert Fathers*, Constable, 193, p. 112.
12. *The Larger Catechism*, A. L.
13. I am indebted to Prof. R. Buick-Knox for this information.
14. OUP p. 126. Peng. p. 135.
15. Peter Toon, *The Correspondence of John Owen*, Cambridge, James Clarke, 1970, p. 148.
16. W. R. Matthews, *Memories and Meanings*, Hodder and Stoughton, 1969, p. 44.
17. Richard Sibbes, *The Soul's Conflict with Itself*, Works, Edinburgh, Grossard, 1862, I, p. 235.
18. This sermon was printed at the time.
19. OUP pp. 128f., 257. Peng. pp. 137f., 273.
20. OUP p. 247. Peng. p. 263.
21. T. S Eliot, 'Little Gidding', *The Complete Poems and Plays*, Faber and Faber, 1961, p. 197.